U.S. Department of Justice
Office of Justice Programs
National Institute of Justice

NIJ

NATIONAL INSTITUTE OF JUSTICE

'04

To the President, the Attorney General, and the Congress:

It is my honor to transmit the National Institute of Justice's annual report on research, development, and evaluation for fiscal year 2004, pursuant to the Omnibus Crime Control and Safe Streets Act (as amended) and the 1988 Anti-Drug Abuse Act.

Respectfully submitted,

Sarah V. Hart

Sarah V. Hart
Director, National Institute of Justice
Washington, D.C.

NATIONAL INSTITUTE OF JUSTICE

Annual Report

U.S. Department of Justice
Office of Justice Programs

810 Seventh Street, N.W.
Washington, DC 20531

Alberto R. Gonzales
Attorney General

Regina B. Schofield
Assistant Attorney General

Sarah V. Hart
Director, National Institute of Justice

This and other publications and products of the
National Institute of Justice can be found at:

National Institute of Justice
http://www.ojp.usdoj.gov/nij

Office of Justice Programs
Partnerships for Safer Communities
http://www.ojp.usdoj.gov

Table of Contents

Timeline 1968–2003

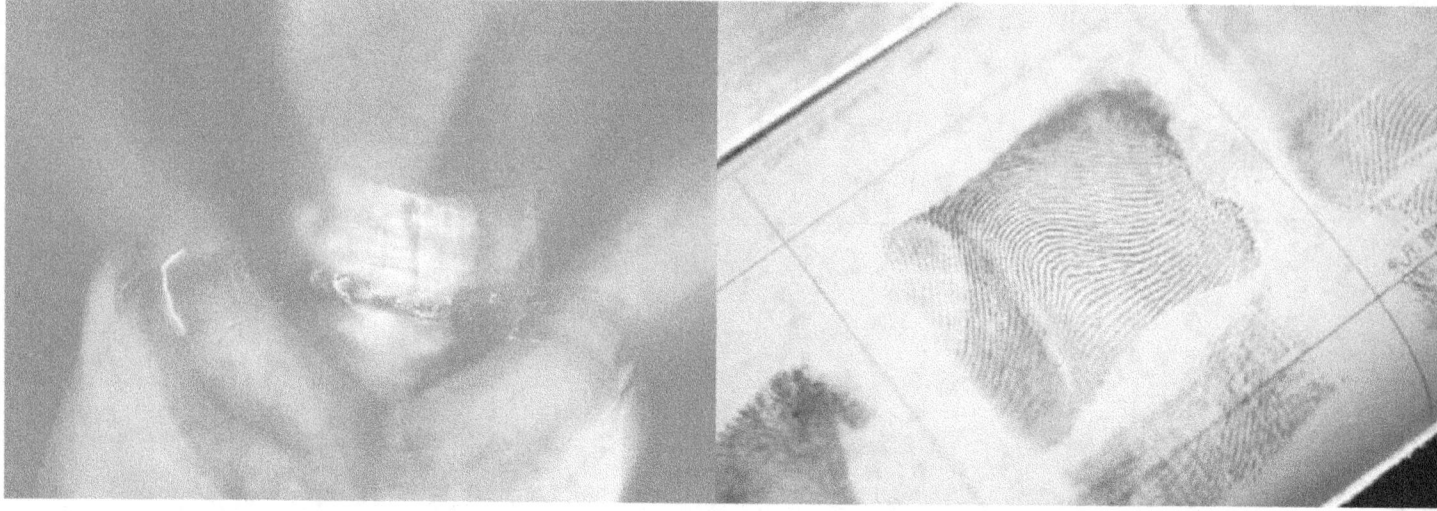

1968	1969	1970	1971	1972	1973	1974	1975	1976

1968 — Congress passes the Omnibus Crime Control and Safe Streets Act, which creates NIJ (then called the National Institute of Law Enforcement and Criminal Justice), to monitor and support Federally funded criminal justice research intended to help State and local governments improve police, courts, and corrections.

1969 — With 35 employees and a budget of $2.5 million, NIJ begins operations. Awards during the first year encompass several key areas: law enforcement communications systems, crime prevention and rehabilitation, technology, and management and organization of the criminal justice system.

1970 — NIJ evaluates methadone maintenance as a means of dealing with drug abuse and related crime.

1971 — NIJ establishes the Law Enforcement Standards Laboratory under the auspices of the National Bureau of Standards to begin filling a long-standing need for scientifically based standards for criminal justice equipment.

1972 — NIJ begins to fund development of soft body armor for police, an initiative destined to save thousands of officers from serious injury and death in subsequent years.

NIJ-funded research on "defensible space" links the physical design of buildings to neighborhoods' vulnerability and leads to models of crime prevention through urban design.

NIJ launches the National Criminal Justice Reference Service.

With NIJ funding, Marvin Wolfgang's study on delinquency in a birth cohort finds that a small proportion of criminals commit most crime.

1973 — Research on jury management shows ways to make trials more efficient, less costly, and less time-consuming for those who serve.

U.S. Parole Commission adopts research-based guidelines for parole decisions; several States follow.

1974 — NIJ publishes findings from the Kansas City (Missouri) Preventive Patrol Experiment, which tested the then-common assumption that by driving more or less randomly in a given area, officers in patrol cars prevented crime, made the public feel more secure, and increased the chances of arresting suspects. Study results indicated that preventive patrol did not necessarily prevent crime or reassure the public. Subsequently, many police departments began issuing officers specific proactive assignments.

1975 — An NIJ-funded study reveals the difficulties victims face in the criminal justice system; recommended reforms lead to the creation of victim assistance programs nationwide.

1976 — Research finds that the time it takes to report a crime—not the speed of the police response—is the major factor influencing the likelihood of arrest.

1977	1978	1979	1980	1981	1982	1983	1984	1985

1977

Research on criminal investigation concludes that the probability of an arrest is largely determined by information obtained by officers first on the crime scene. If specific types of information are not collected at this time, the chances of solving a case remain low, regardless of the intensity of a followup investigation. These findings lead to the identification of "solvability factors," which become guides for prioritizing followup investigations.

NIJ initiates the crime laboratory proficiency testing program to measure the analytical accuracy of evidence analysis nationwide.

NIJ launches research on alternatives to traditional parole.

1978

NIJ examines new techniques for detecting and identifying explosives.

Under an NIJ grant, more than 300 forensic laboratory specialists are taught how to analyze types of evidence posing the greatest difficulties for forensic examination.

1979

NIJ launches *Crime and Justice*, a scholarly series edited by Michael Tonry and published by the University of Chicago Press.

1980

NIJ funds an experiment in Minneapolis, Minnesota, to explore options for police responses to domestic violence calls.

NIJ publishes findings of research exploring why career criminals so often "beat the system," prompting the emergence of career criminal prosecution programs.

1981

Results of the NIJ-sponsored Newark, New Jersey, Foot Patrol Experiment are released. This and subsequent experiments focusing on problem-oriented policing tested whether various forms of foot patrol, door-to-door contact, and other positive contacts between police and the community could reduce fear of crime and improve neighborhood life. This research foreshadowed the development of community policing.

1982

"Broken Windows," by James Q. Wilson and George L. Kelling, appears in the *Atlantic Monthly*.

Research shows a link between drug use and crime. The findings set the stage for the 1987 launch of Federal-local partnerships to collect data and measure drug use among arrestees.

1983

Research on pretrial release is published and suggests that an objective method exists to identify which defendants are most likely to appear for trial. Courts begin implementing formal pretrial release guidelines modeled after the original research.

1984

Research finds that the best predictor of success of drug treatment is the length of time one stays in treatment.

Minneapolis experiment indicates that spending the night in jail appears to significantly cut the risk of repeat violence against the same victim, a finding that motivates many police departments to require an arrest in domestic violence situations.

1985

Research on probation in California finds that routine probation provides insufficient punishment for offenders and inadequate protection for the community. This finding helps spur interest in intermediate sanctions (e.g., boot camps, house arrest, intensive supervision, and electronic monitoring).

1986	1987	1988	1989	1990	1991	1992	1993	1994

NIJ begins support for the development of DNA technology applicable to criminal justice.

NIJ initiates the analysis of drug use by arrestees through its Drug Use Forecasting program (renamed the Arrestee Drug Abuse Monitoring program in 1998).

NIJ designates white-collar crime as a priority research area. Subsequently, the Institute funds major studies on savings and loan fraud, insurance and securities fraud, money laundering, computer crime, telemarketing fraud, environmental crime, and public corruption.

First drug court is established (in Miami, Florida). NIJ begins an evaluation that eventually shows that drug courts hold promise for reducing drug-related recidivism.

NIJ initiates several efforts to improve DNA testing.

NIJ and the John D. and Catherine T. MacArthur Foundation join to establish the Project on Human Development in Chicago Neighborhoods, which begins examining the social development of 7,000 individuals from birth to age 24 and gauging influences on delinquency and crime.

NIJ provides technical assistance to expand private sector involvement in prison industries programs.

Research confirms a "cycle of violence," in which abused, neglected children are more likely to become involved in later criminal behavior.

The first "Three Strikes" laws are enacted.

Understanding and Preventing Violence is released. This report from the National Academy of Sciences lays the groundwork for the next decade of research at NIJ on violence and victimization.

NIJ creates a system of regional technology centers (the National Law Enforcement and Corrections Technology Centers) to respond to the need for technology information and assistance.

Congress passes the Violent Crime Control and Law Enforcement Act.

1995	1996	1997	1998	1999	2000	2001	2002	2003

NIJ initiates major research and evaluation efforts in program areas included in the 1994 Crime Act—community policing, violence against women, sentencing and corrections, and drug courts.

NIJ awards funds to enhance State and local DNA laboratory processing capabilities, publishes a report documenting case studies in which DNA evidence presented after trial led to the release of inmates convicted of violent felonies, and sponsors a national conference on the future of DNA evidence.

NIJ issues the first annual report to Congress on stalking and domestic violence.

NIJ establishes the Crime Mapping Research Center and the International Center.

NIJ publishes *Preventing Crime: What Works, What Doesn't, What's Promising.*

Science magazine publishes findings on the influence of neighborhoods based on research from the Project on Human Development in Chicago Neighborhoods.

At the request of the Attorney General, NIJ forms the National Commission on the Future of DNA Evidence, leading to a series of recommendations on the use of DNA in the criminal justice system.

In collaboration with other agencies, NIJ works with policymakers, judges, and correctional officials to address challenges posed by the reentry of large numbers of prisoners into communities.

NIJ prepares guidelines on crime scene investigation, death investigation, and eyewitness evidence using expert panels to identify best practices.

NIJ publishes the 4-volume series *Criminal Justice 2000*, essays on current and emerging trends in criminal justice.

The National Commission on the Future of DNA Evidence produces a pocket guide on collecting DNA evidence at crime scenes. Copies are printed for every sworn law enforcement officer in the Nation.

Results from the National Violence Against Women Survey, co-sponsored by NIJ and the Centers for Disease Control and Prevention, show that more than half of surveyed women reported being physically assaulted at some point in their lives, and nearly two-thirds of women who reported being raped, assaulted, or stalked were victimized by intimate partners.

NIJ responds to the 9-11 attacks with onsite assistance, including search and rescue tools and technology and protective gear. NIJ speeds up production of equipment guides for first responders.

NIJ develops a technique to distinguish between crack and powder cocaine use in test subjects.

Six cities are found to have reduced firearms violence through action research initiated by NIJ.

Ground-breaking research provides the first comprehensive national look at rape and sexual assault on college campuses.

NIJ reports to Congress on the viability of using various less-lethal weapons aboard commercial aircraft as a means of thwarting an onboard attack.

NIJ completes a comprehensive report to the Attorney General on the extent and causes of delays in analyzing DNA evidence. Six report recommendations become the foundation of "Advancing Justice Through DNA Technology," the President's DNA initiative.

NIJ sponsors the development of biometrics as a tool for security and criminal justice. Face and iris recognition technologies are tested in prisons and schools.

A trainer's manual on eyewitness evidence is released. The manual presents effective techniques for interviewing witnesses and conducting lineups.

Highlights of the Year

In 2003, crime victimizations in the United States approached 24 million—about 5.4 million were violent crimes, and more than 18 million were property crimes.[1] In addition to the emotional and mental losses for victims, crime exacts an enormous financial toll, with gross annual losses of nearly $16 billion.[2]

The primary challenge for criminal justice professionals today is not from the number of crimes, however, but from the changing nature of the crime landscape. Although traditional criminal activities such as juvenile delinquency, gangs, burglary, and violent crimes remain problems for many communities, law enforcement agencies now face such new threats as the evolving globalization of crime, possible terrorism, and cybercrime.

At the same time, advances in technology—such as lower costs for the analysis of DNA samples—are changing how evidence is collected and crimes are investigated, as well as how judges and attorneys handle court cases.

The National Institute of Justice (NIJ) is the research, development, and evaluation agency of the U.S. Department of Justice and is dedicated to researching crime control and justice issues. NIJ provides objective, independent, evidence-based knowledge and tools to meet the challenges of crime and justice, particularly at the State and local levels. The agency often forms partnerships with other Federal agencies, scientific and academic institutions and experts, law enforcement and corrections agencies, and professional organizations. Such joint ventures bring together the best minds, experience, and resources to explore emerging technologies, evaluate programs, develop standards, facilitate research, disseminate findings, and tackle pressing issues involving public safety, justice, law enforcement, and corrections.

[1] Catalano, S.M., *Criminal Victimization, 2003*, Washington, DC: U.S. Department of Justice, Bureau of Justice Statistics, September 2004 (NCJ 205455), available at http://www.ojp. usdoj.gov/bjs/pub/pdf/cv03.pdf.

[2] From the National Crime Victimization Survey of 2002, published on the World Wide Web in *Criminal Victimization in the United States—Statistical Tables*, December 2003 (NCJ 200561): Table 82, "Personal and property crimes, 2002," available at http://www.ojp.usdoj.gov/bjs/pub/pdf/ cvus/current/cv0282.pdf.

NIJ is committed to making DNA analysis a routine and affordable tool for State and local law enforcement.

The changing landscape of crime and justice

Addressing new types of crime as well as new versions of old patterns of crime requires innovative approaches. NIJ has always been at the forefront of innovation and change. For example, during the 1970's the agency pioneered development of bullet-resistant vests for police and during the 1980's sponsored research that led to new practices for prosecuting career criminals. By the turn of the century, remarkable advances in forensics began changing how crimes are investigated and criminals are prosecuted.

The most prominent of these advances is the collection and analysis of DNA evidence. Today NIJ is supporting development of cheaper, faster ways to use DNA samples as forensic evidence in all types of crimes, not just homicide and sexual assault. For example, police have discovered that biological evidence collected from a burglary crime scene can lead to arrest and conviction of career criminals capable of more serious offenses.

Science and the law. NIJ is committed to making DNA analysis a routine and affordable tool for State and local law enforcement. In 2003, the President announced the "Advancing Justice Through DNA Technology" initiative to provide $1 billion over 5 years to use DNA identification to solve crimes, to improve crime labs and train investigators, and to stimulate research and development. Congress passed this legislation in 2004, and NIJ launched an interagency partnership and a Web site about the initiative—http://www.DNA.gov.

As more offender DNA samples are collected and law enforcement becomes better trained and equipped to collect DNA samples at crime scenes, the backlog of samples awaiting testing throughout the criminal justice system has increased to more than 542,000. In response, NIJ awarded $66.5 million in grants to reduce the DNA testing backlog and build crime lab capacity.

Globalization. Another factor that contributes to the changing landscape of crime is globalization. Business and commerce see the impact of globalization every day. Its impact on crime may not be as readily visible, but the effect is just as dramatic. Human trafficking, for example, involves an estimated 700,000 people each year, most of them women and children taken from their homes and forced into labor and/or prostitution under the pretense of legitimate employment.[3] Since 1998, NIJ has participated in and funded a range of research projects and related initiatives to understand and stop human trafficking; a new research solicitation was posted in January 2005.

Most people think of human trafficking in terms of people being smuggled into the United States. But not all cases involve victims from other countries. One-third of the victims involved in a 2003–2004 NIJ-sponsored study of 12 cases in various U.S. locations were recruited *within* the United States.[4] The researchers examined workers in several fields, including prostitution, domestic service, entertainment, agriculture, factories, and restaurants. They found that success in combating this problem depends on close collaboration among Federal authorities, local government agencies, nongovernmental organizations, and service providers and that the special inspection powers and experience of U.S. Department of Labor investigators are a valuable and underutilized resource for gathering evidence on trafficking and forced labor cases.

On a more positive side, globalization has also opened up countries formerly within the Soviet orbit to democracy, permitting them to seek help from other nations. For example, Ukraine received guidance and research assistance from NIJ to find ways to reform its criminal justice system and eliminate entrenched corruption. Working with the U.S. State Department, NIJ launched a series of projects that prompted Ukraine to begin reforming its penal code and take steps to enact legislation on intellectual property crime and the global problems of Internet piracy and trafficking.[5]

Research on organized crime in Asia and intellectual property theft around the world was conducted for NIJ during 2004; findings are expected to be published in 2005.

[3] Albanese, J., "Commercial Sexual Exploitation of Children: Assessing What We Know and Its Implications for Research and Practice," *International Journal of Comparative Criminology,* 4(1) (2004): 24–47.

[4] Bales, K., and S. Lize, "Human Trafficking in the United States," final report to the National Institute of Justice, February 2005, available at http://www.ncjrs.org.

[5] See *The Prediction and Control of Organized Crime: The Experience of Post-Soviet Ukraine,* Finckenauer, J.O., and J.L. Schrock, eds., Somerset, NJ: Transaction Publishers, 2004.

In this report

Helping the justice system adapt to the changing landscape of crime, prosecution, corrections, and public safety requires strategic thinking about how to apply limited resources. New and stable strategies and resources are needed not only for the day-to-day work of enforcement, prevention, adjudication, and incarceration, but also for forward-looking research and development.

Most State and local governments, however, cannot devote funds to criminal justice research and development. The majority of the country's 16,000 law enforcement agencies, for example, have very small staffs and limited resources that must be directed toward local crime problems. As a Federal partner, NIJ is poised to continue its role as a major source of criminal justice research and development funding for State and local agencies, as well as a source of the latest information about what works.

The *2004 Annual Report* demonstrates how NIJ is making a difference in five broad areas—solving crimes, improving law enforcement, ensuring justice, improving corrections, and increasing community safety. The timeline (see page v) places these activities within four decades of historical context. The appendixes provide detailed breakdowns of the year's financial operations, research and development grants, and public information dissemination through printed publications and the Internet.

Solving Crimes

Forensic science, especially the analysis of DNA, is radically changing how crimes are investigated. Using the smallest remnants of evidence, forensic scientists can hasten arrests, prevent further crime, and exonerate the innocent. NIJ supports a number of projects that advance forensic science. DNA analysis is the best known, but progress continues to be made in other areas such as digital evidence, handwriting analysis, and ballistic signature analysis.

DNA analysis

Although the cost of analyzing DNA is decreasing, most U.S. law enforcement agencies still do not routinely collect DNA evidence, especially "invisible evidence" such as the sweat in the lining of a suspect's baseball cap.

NIJ is working in partnership with the President's DNA Initiative (discussed on page 2) to build the Nation's capacity to:

- Use DNA as a routine law enforcement tool.

- Eliminate current backlogs of convicted offender and casework DNA samples.

- Use DNA to identify missing persons and provide closure to families.

- Benefit from future developments in DNA technology.

A major part of NIJ's portfolio focuses on using DNA to solve crimes that have reached a dead end. DNA technology and databases with DNA profiles of convicted offenders are inspiring law enforcement agencies to reevaluate their cold cases. For example, in 1990, in Goldsboro, North Carolina, a man broke into several homes, raped three elderly women, and murdered two of the women and one of their husbands. This "Night Stalker" case had no suspects, though the intruder's DNA was entered into a database. More than 10 years later, the intruder's DNA matched with that of an offender whose DNA was entered into the database after he was convicted of a shooting. The match solved the Goldsboro "Night Stalker" case.

Justice professionals face two significant hurdles in analyzing DNA: a backlog of samples from convicted offenders and a backlog of forensic samples from cases. The convicted-offender backlog includes as many as 300,000 unanalyzed DNA samples from offenders convicted of crimes, with more than 500,000 samples yet to be taken. According to the best estimates, the forensic casework backlog includes approximately 52,000 homicide cases, 169,000 sexual assault cases, and 264,000 property crime cases.

Lack of funding is frequently cited as the reason why law enforcement agencies do not make greater use of DNA analysis. To help with the financial strain, NIJ awarded $39.7 million to 39 States in 2003 to analyze DNA from crime scene evidence and improve the capacity of crime labs. In 2004, NIJ awarded $66.5 million to State and local crime labs to help reduce the estimated 543,000 criminal cases with biological evidence waiting for DNA testing and to enhance the capacity of DNA laboratories.[6]

Ongoing NIJ research is helping police chiefs understand how DNA evidence from property crime offenders can solve more serious personal crimes. Police departments in Miami-Dade County (Florida), New York (New York), and Palm Beach (Florida) are achieving dramatic results by analyzing biological evidence collected from property crime scenes. In New York, one DNA profile uncovered a five-burglary serial offender. Many profiles from burglaries link to serious violent crimes such as sexual assault and robbery.

The cost of DNA testing depends on the number of samples tested, the type of DNA testing needed, and the costs involved for police to collect biological evidence at property crime scenes and pursue investigative leads generated by DNA. But these costs must be weighed against the losses incurred by the public from crime and the cost for investigators to follow clues the traditional way.

NIJ's forensics research and development portfolio is designed to create innovative tools and technologies crime lab personnel can use to reduce costs while increasing efficiency and accuracy. In 2004, NIJ awarded funds for a variety of research projects to develop or explore:

[6] Awards totaling $38.1 million are for reducing backlogged DNA casework; awards totaling $28.4 million are for laboratory enhancement.

Topics from NIJ research that appeared in peer-reviewed journals in 2004 include: mitochondrial DNA; mini-STR's; characterization of DNA damage in bloodstains; Y-chromosome studies for use in investigations of crimes involving males; a microdevice system for forensic DNA analysis; and insect DNA studies, which are useful in homicide investigations for determining the time since death.

- Better ways to identify and separate male and female DNA in sexual assault cases.

- New DNA markers to help pinpoint the source of DNA evidence.

- Methods to determine the tissue origin of biological evidence.

- Miniaturized forensic DNA testing devices with potential field use.

- Improved methods for examining nonhuman DNA, which is often associated with crime scene evidence and may play a key role in an investigation.

NIJ disseminates research findings through several mechanisms, including traditional peer-reviewed scientific literature and sharing information about products developed through NIJ research. For example, in 2004, a rapid method for testing mitochondrial DNA was commercialized. The method, called the Linear Array Assay, was previously used to examine skeletal remains recovered from mass graves in Croatia.

Technology transfer activities familiarize practitioners with newly developed methods. In 2004, an NIJ grantee conducted a workshop that provided hands-on training in methods developed by the grantee to analyze plant DNA.

For more information

- The President's initiative, Advancing Justice Through DNA Technology, is described in detail on http://www.DNA.gov.

- *DNA in "Minor" Crimes Yields Major Benefits in Public Safety*, In Short—Toward Criminal Justice Solutions, Washington, DC: U.S. Department of Justice, National Institute of Justice, November 2004 (NCJ 207203), available at http://www.ncjrs.org/pdffiles1/nij/207203.pdf.

- *Using DNA to Solve Cold Cases*, Special Report, Washington, DC: U.S. Department of Justice, National Institute of Justice, July 2002 (NCJ 194197), available at http://www.ncjrs.org/pdffiles1/nij/194197.pdf.

A "questioned" document is any signature, handwriting, typewriting, or other mark whose source or authenticity is doubtful or in dispute. Letters, checks, driver's licenses, contracts, wills, voter registrations, passports, petitions, threatening letters, suicide notes, and lottery tickets are the most commonly questioned documents.

Other forensics

NIJ's portfolio of projects related to forensic evidence includes studies to interpret handwriting and collect and process digital evidence.

Questioned documents. Questioned document examination is concerned with handwriting analysis and technical aspects of document writing. In a 1993 landmark case, *Daubert v. Merrell Dow Pharmaceuticals, Inc.,* the U.S. Supreme Court found that the forensic techniques on which experts testify should be based on rigorous scientific procedures (such as peer reviews and replicated findings) rather than on what the Court called "generally accepted" practices.[7] For many years handwriting analysis determined the authenticity of questioned documents, but until *Daubert,* the forensic methods for analyzing questioned documents had not been rigorously tested. After *Daubert,* NIJ became interested in work being done for the U.S. Postal Service by scientists at the State University of New York at Buffalo (SUNY). Using a computer algorithm, their system was able to read handwritten addresses on envelopes.

Through NIJ funding, SUNY researchers have developed a software system called CEDAR-FOX to perform tasks normally done by forensic document examiners. In early demonstrations, CEDAR-FOX correctly identified the writer in 96 percent of the samples tested. In 2004, NIJ funded further development and refinement of CEDAR-FOX to increase its capability as an operational tool for questioned document specialists.

Digital evidence and electronic crime. Hacking and disruption due to "phishing" (e-mail spoofs, fraudulent Web sites), child pornography, and any number of other crimes committed using computers and the Internet have led businesses and law enforcement agencies to invest in computer forensics.

7 Noting that the "general acceptance" test established in *Frye v. United States,* 293 F. 1013, 1014 (D.C. Cir. 1923), was superceded by the adoption of the Federal Rules of Evidence, the Court held that "nothing in the text of … [Federal Rule of Evidence 702] establishes 'general acceptance' as an absolute prerequisite to admissibility." *Daubert v. Merrell Dow Pharmaceuticals, Inc.,* 509 U.S. 579, 588, 113 S.Ct. 2786, 2794 (1993).

In 2004, NIJ released the second in its series of guides for investigating electronic crime (see "For more information," below) and continued testing the accuracy of various forensic tools to investigate and solve electronic crimes. One notable result in 2004: NIJ, through funding to the National Institute of Standards and Technology, Office of Law Enforcement Standards, released test results of software write block tools and disk imaging tools. The latter were used in the proceedings against suspected 9-11 terrorist Zacharias Moussaoui.

With its partners in the Critical Incident Technology Initiative (the Federal Bureau of Investigation [FBI], the U.S. Customs and Border Protection Service, and the U.S. Department of Defense), NIJ developed a system in which software from various data sources is compiled into a data set—the National Software Reference Library. Investigators can compare digital evidence from the hard drive of a computer seized as evidence with software in the reference library data set, which reduces investigative time. The current version (2.4) was released in 2004.

For more information

- *Test Results for Disk Imaging Tools: dd Provided with FreeBSD 4.4,* Special Report, Washington, DC: U.S. Department of Justice, National Institute of Justice, January 2004 (NCJ 203095), available at http://www.ncjrs.org/pdffiles1/ nij/203095.pdf; and *Test Results for Software Write Block Tools: RCMP HDL VO.8,* Special Report, Washington, DC: U.S. Department of Justice, National Institute of Justice, February 2004 (NCJ 203196), available at http://www. ncjrs.org/pdffiles1/nij/203196.pdf.

- *Forensic Examination of Digital Evidence: A Guide for Law Enforcement,* Special Report, Washington, DC: U.S. Department of Justice, National Institute of Justice, April 2004 (NCJ 199408), available at http://www.ncjrs.org/ pdffiles1/nij/199408.pdf.

Ballistic analysis. Through NIJ funding, researchers at Intelligent Automation, Inc., have developed a 3-dimensional (3-D) imaging system for examining the markings that are imprinted on a bullet as it travels through the barrel of a gun. This system can automatically obtain 3-D data from bullets, store the information in a database, extract a "signature" associated with the data, and evaluate the degree of similarity between signatures. Forensic Technology, Inc., commercialized the system in 2004 and currently is moving the new 3-D-based technology from the research stage to the marketplace for law enforcement and forensic use.

Training crime scene investigators

Securing a crime scene and collecting evidence have always formed the backbone of successful investigation and prosecution. These skills are arguably even more critical in the changed landscape of 2004, where rapid technological advances have greatly expanded the amount of information that can be obtained from physical evidence.

NIJ formed the Technical Working Group on Crime Scene Investigation to compile comprehensive technical training manuals for crime scene investigation. These manuals continue to be NIJ "best sellers." In June 2004, NIJ released the latest manual: *Crime Scene Investigation: A Reference for Law Enforcement Training.*[8]

[8] *Crime Scene Investigation: A Reference for Law Enforcement Training,* Special Report, Washington, DC: U.S. Department of Justice, National Institute of Justice, June 2004 (NCJ 200160), available at http://www.ncjrs.org/pdffiles1/200160.pdf.

Improving Law Enforcement

Of all the research NIJ has added to its portfolio over the years, the body of work on policing may be the largest. Community-oriented policing. Use of force. Pursuit management. Less-lethal technology. Police use of discretion. NIJ-sponsored research and development have contributed to a better understanding of these and other topics.

During 2004, NIJ expanded two areas of study that directly affect the quality of law enforcement: interoperability (interagency communications) and the impact of human factors on policing.

Another important area of NIJ research involves protecting the safety of law enforcement personnel through development of lighter, more comfortable body armor and standards for its performance. Bullet-resistant vests have saved more than 2,800 officers' lives over the past 30 years.

Interoperability

One of NIJ's most prominent research missions involves finding ways for multiple public safety agencies to communicate with one another during a critical incident, such as a high-speed pursuit, natural disaster, or terrorist attack. Police, fire, medical, and other personnel at the scene and across jurisdictions often cannot talk to all parties because their radios are incompatible. First responders must share information instantly and effortlessly or lives can be lost. They need interoperability.

Before interoperability was recognized at the national level as a critical public safety concern, NIJ's AGILE program already had laid the foundation for developing interoperability policy and standards through its support for technology research that is now universally recognized.[9] With this foundation in place, the agency's interoperability activities have moved into the realm of practice—identifying, adopting, and developing practical communications solutions that include open architecture standards for voice, data, image, and video systems.

[9] Founded by NIJ in 1998, AGILE stands for Advanced Generation of Interoperability for Law Enforcement.

In 2004, the U.S. Department of Homeland Security reenergized the SAFECOM program to become the primary coordinator for all of the Federal Government's interoperability programs.[10] As a result, NIJ shifted to a primary focus on interoperability for law enforcement and renamed AGILE "CommTech." CommTech will continue to sponsor interoperability research and evaluation, standards development, and outreach to help policymakers and public safety leaders make informed, cost-effective decisions.[11]

In September 2004, NIJ's Office of Science and Technology (OST) and the U.S. Department of Homeland Security's Science and Technology Directorate sponsored their first annual joint conference, "Technologies for Public Safety in Critical Incident Response," held in New Orleans, Louisiana. The conference allowed first responders, industry leaders, academicians, and elected Federal, State, and local officials to exchange ideas concerning common critical incident technology needs. The 2005 conference is scheduled for October 31–November 2, 2005, in San Diego, California.

OST also cosponsors the Capital Wireless Integrated Network (CapWIN), the first integrated, multi-State public safety wireless network in the Nation. CapWIN connects public safety personnel from more than 35 agencies in the Washington, DC, metropolitan area through a messaging switch located in Alexandria, Virginia. System testing and expansion to laptops and PDA's are ongoing.

For more information

- NIJ's National Law Enforcement and Corrections Technology Center (NLECTC) provides CommTech and other interoperability support and information. See the CommTech Web site at http://www.nlectc.org/agile/justnet.html.

- "'Why Can't We Talk?' When Lives are at Stake," fact sheet and video available online at http://www.justnet.org/assistance/interopfactsheet.html.

- "A CapWIN-Win Solution," *TechBeat*, Winter 2004, available at http://www.justnet.org/techbeat/winter2004/CapWinWint04.pdf.

---

[10] SAFECOM is the Federal umbrella program that helps local, tribal, State, and Federal public safety agencies improve public safety response through interoperable wireless communications. Prior to 2004, NIJ's AGILE program had played a primary role in coordinating the public safety community's interoperability policies. For more information, see http://www.safecomprogram.gov.

[11] NIJ's Office of Law Enforcement Standards formed partnerships in 2004 with several agencies and organizations to develop open architecture standards for public safety communication systems. See http://www.eeel.nist.gov/oles/public_safety.html for more information.

Darrel W. Stephens
Chief of Police,
Charlotte-Mecklenburg,
North Carolina

"The art and science of policing has improved enormously over the past 35 years because of the research the National Institute of Justice has encouraged and supported. The result is a safer America."

Human factors

NIJ's research on police behavior over the past several decades includes examinations of how officers use discretion and force, how they work with the community to solve entrenched crime problems, and how they and their families handle the stress of police work. In 2004, NIJ expanded this research base to include the impact of fatigue on human performance and the role of intuitive behaviors or "gut responses."

Fatigue. It is well-established that long work hours have negative effects on a person's general health, the tendency to have a driving accident or an on-the-job injury, and cognitive performance. Many workers whose activities affect public safety—for example, airline pilots, truck drivers, and nurses—must abide by working hour standards and restrictions designed to prevent excess fatigue. Police officers do not.

The research is a long way from fully explaining how officer fatigue affects police work, but it is clear that law enforcement suffers when officers are fatigued due to overtime, shift work, court appearances, and the emotional and physical demands of the job. About a third of police officers work 20 or more hours of overtime per month and more than half "moonlight" at other jobs.[12]

Intuition. Experienced officers sometimes intuitively react to danger signals before they are consciously aware of them. Police intuition also plays an important role in directing suspicion, guiding investigations, and interrogating. Intuitive judgments are made more quickly than formal decisionmaking and are influenced by social context, expectations, and attitudes.

NIJ is forming a research agenda to explore police decisionmaking and how it can be improved. In 2004, the agency put together a multidisciplinary collaboration with the FBI, the American Psychological Association, the Affect and Biobehavioral Regulation Program at the National Institute of Mental Health, and the National Institute for Occupational Safety and Health at the Centers for Disease Control and Prevention. A conference on police intuition was held in June.

[12] Vila, B., and D.J. Kenny, *Tired Cops: The Importance of Managing Police Fatigue*, Flemington, NJ: Police Executive Research Forum, 2000.

The U.S. Department of Justice sponsored a 1-day national summit on body armor in March 2004. Attendees included representatives from Federal, State, tribal, and local law enforcement; law enforcement associations; manufacturers of bullet-resistant fabric and equipment; and standards and testing organizations. Participants discussed the NIJ testing and standards program—whether it should remain voluntary, the ongoing testing of Zylon®-based vests, and other matters.

For more information

- Vila, B., and D.J. Kenney, "Tired Cops: The Prevalence and Potential Consequences of Police Fatigue," *NIJ Journal* 248 (March 2002): 16–21, available at http://www.ncjrs.org/pdffiles1/jr000248d.pdf.

- "The Nature and Influence of Intuition in Law Enforcement: Integration of Theory and Practice," conference sponsored by NIJ and the FBI Training Academy in Arlington, Virginia, June 2004. The agenda and readings are available from the American Psychological Association Web site at http://www.apa.org/ppo/issues/intuition.html.

Protecting law enforcement personnel

NIJ has sponsored several initiatives in recent years supporting technology and training to improve the safety and survivability of law enforcement personnel.

Body armor. More than 2,800 police officers' lives have been saved by body armor since the mid-1970's, when NIJ began testing and developing performance standards for ballistic- and stab-resistant body armor. Most police departments only purchase vests that are certified as meeting NIJ standards.

After a reported failure of an NIJ-compliant vest in 2003, the U.S. Department of Justice launched an initiative to assess body armor reliability and certification. NIJ was tasked to evaluate Zylon®-based bullet-resistant vests and released a report in March 2004 and a supplemental report in December.[13] Although the cause of the vest failure remains undetermined, testing is still ongoing. Preliminary findings from the second phase of testing are anticipated in 2005.[14]

Training manuals and equipment guides. NIJ supports research into law enforcement equipment and technology and develops training manuals and guides to ensure public and officer safety. After 9-11, the agency published several guides for the selection of personal protective and other equipment for emergency first responders.[15]

[13] *Status Report to the Attorney General on Body Armor Safety Initiative Testing and Activities,* Washington, DC: U.S. Department of Justice, National Institute of Justice, March 11, 2004 (NCJ 204534), and Supplement I to the report, December 27, 2004 (NCJ 207605). Both are available at http://www.ojp.usdoj.gov/nij/pubs-sum/207605.htm.

[14] The first phase of testing revealed promising data about ballistic-resistant materials' degradation over time that could lead to improved performance testing methodology.

[15] These guides can be downloaded from http://nij.ncjrs.org/publications/pubs_db.asp. Click on "Search NIJ Publications" and select "Officer Protection" for a complete listing.

In 2004, NIJ released a report on impact munitions—less-lethal devices used to subdue potentially dangerous individuals and to disperse unruly crowds. Impact munitions can help law enforcement officers resolve potentially violent encounters without using deadly force. These devices can compromise officer or public safety, however, if they are not applied properly. NIJ researchers surveyed 106 agencies about 373 incidents in which 969 projectiles were fired. More than 90 percent of the incidents were resolved without lethal force.

Another report released in 2004, *Department of Defense Nonlethal Weapons and Equipment Review: A Research Guide for Civil Law Enforcement and Corrections,* provides a detailed equipment review of the department's nonlethal weapons program and currently used nonlethal technologies. Five categories of nonlethal technologies are reviewed: chemicals, electrical devices, blunt impact munitions, directed energy, and miscellaneous or hybrid systems.

Defeating bomb threats. Current methods to confirm or deny the presence of a bomb or "improvised explosive device" (IED) place officers or bomb-disposal technicians at risk and are expensive and cumbersome to deploy. Since 1999, NIJ has supported research into the use of robot technology to disarm explosive devices. The agency recently published a summary evaluation comparing the Vanguard Robot's performance to that of other bomb-disposal robots. The Vanguard has many features required by law enforcement (such as affordability) and has performed better than comparable systems on tasks commonly encountered by technicians. However, it did not satisfy the requirements for speed and mission duration. Evaluators suggested enhancements that would increase Vanguard's benefits to practitioners, and the manufacturer modified it accordingly. NIJ is funding an evaluation of the new model.

In October 2004, NIJ formally solicited concept papers for developing new tools and technologies that law enforcement personnel could use to defeat an IED threat, specifically in three areas of concern: confirming the presence of a vehicle bomb, neutralizing a vehicle bomb, and disposing of a bomb. For example, law enforcement needs cost-effective, portable means to confirm or deny that a bomb is inside a vehicle without endangering officers, such as a handheld device that can detect an IED from 300 meters away or that is conveyed by a small robot. The solicitation closed in December 2004, and the agency is reviewing proposed concepts.[16]

For more information

- Information on body armor testing and evaluation is available from NLECTC at http://www.justnet.org/testing/justnet.html. The U.S. Department of Justice's Body Armor Safety Initiative is described at http://vests.ojp.gov/index.jsp.

- Hubbs, K., and D. Klinger, *Impact Munitions Use: Types, Targets, Effects,* Research for Practice, Washington, DC: U.S. Department of Justice, National Institute of Justice, October 2004 (NCJ 206089), available at http://www.ncjrs.org/pdffiles1/nij/206089.pdf.[17]

- *Department of Defense Nonlethal Weapons and Equipment Review: A Research Guide for Civil Law Enforcement and Corrections,* Special Report, Washington, DC: U.S. Department of Justice, National Institute of Justice, October 2004 (NCJ 205293), available at http://www.ncjrs.org/pdffiles1/nij/205293.pdf.

- *Vanguard Robot Assessment,* In Short—Toward Criminal Justice Solutions, Washington, DC: U.S. Department of Justice, National Institute of Justice, July 2004 (NCJ 204637), available at http://www.ncjrs.org/pdffiles1/nij/204637.pdf.

[16] The solicitation is posted at http://www.ncjrs.org/pdffiles1/nij/sl000680.pdf.

[17] The full grant report, "Impact Munitions Data Base of Use and Effects," February 2004 (NCJ 204433), is available at http://www.ncjrs.org/pdffiles1/nij/grants/204433.pdf.

Ensuring Justice

NIJ has supported several key innovations that have improved court procedures while protecting the public and ensuring justice. The projects were designed to stop the revolving door through which criminals come into court, are sentenced and serve or receive probation, return to the community, commit new crimes, and come back to court. They were also intended to break the cycles of drugs and domestic violence and to make courts more responsive to the needs of their communities.

The Nation's first community court, the Midtown Community Court in Manhattan, New York, is an example of a court that focuses on relatively low-level crimes that lower the morale of the community. The Miami-Dade County drug court, pioneered in the 1990's, continues to be an example of an effective alternative court for dealing with drug offenders. NIJ-funded evaluations of both of these court programs found them to have promise.[18]

Courts that help stop drug abuse

Since 1989, more than 1,500 courts have implemented or are planning to implement a drug court.[19] In these settings, officers of the court (judges, prosecutors, defense counsel) combine their influence with substance abuse treatment specialists, probation officers, educational and vocational experts, and community leaders to pressure offenders to face their drug problems.

Acceptance into a drug court program varies by court, but most drug courts require that the charge before the court involve a nonviolent offense and that the offender has no previous record of violence, is not mentally ill or suicidal, and has a substance abuse problem.

Offenders who enter drug court typically must follow strict rules. For example, they may be required to live at home, submit to weekly drug screenings, report to court four times a week for counseling and therapy, get and keep gainful employment, and agree to unannounced "knock and talk" visits from a police officer or an officer of the court.

18 Sviridoff, M., D.B. Rottman, R. Weidner, F. Cheesman, R. Curtis, R. Hansen, and B.J. Ostrom, "Dispensing Justice Locally: The Impact, Costs, and Benefits of the Midtown Community Court," final report to the National Institute of Justice, 2002 (NCJ 196397), available at http://www.ncjrs.org/pdffiles1/nij/grants/196397.pdf; Anderson, D., "In New York City, a 'Community Court' and a New Legal Culture," final report to the National Institute of Justice, 1996 (NCJ 158613), available at http://www.ncjrs.org/pdffiles/commcrt.pdf; and Goldkamp, J.S., and D. Weiland, "Assessing the Impact of Dade County's Felony Drug Court," final report to the National Institute of Justice, 1993 (NCJ 145302). The Law Offices of the Public Defender for the Eleventh Judicial Circuit of Florida maintains a Web page about the Miami-Dade Drug Court at http://www.pdmiami.com/drug_court.htm. Also see Rothman, D.B., "Community Courts: Prospects and Limits," NIJ Journal 231 (August 1996): 46–51, available at http://ncjrs.org/pdffiles/nijjcomm.pdf.

19 Bureau of Justice Assistance, "Drug Court Discretionary Grant Program: FY 2005 Resource Guide for Drug Court Applicants," U.S. Department of Justice, Bureau of Justice Assistance, retrieved March 17, 2005, from the World Wide Web at http://www.ojp.usdoj.gov/BJA/grant/05DrugCtResGuide.pdf.

Dyer County, Tennessee,
General Sessions Judge
Charles V. Moore, Jr.
quoted in the *Dyersburg State Gazette*,
July 26, 2003

"I've sent a lot of people to rehab, and if they successfully complete it, I see very few of them back."

The drug court judge can adjust rewards and punishments in accordance with how well an offender abides by the rules of the court and participates in the rehab program. For example, if an offender continues to test negative on urine tests, the court may relax the terms of his or her probation.

One NIJ study of 38 drug courts found that out of 17,000 graduates nationwide, 16 percent had been rearrested and charged with a felony 1 year after they graduated from drug court and 28 percent 2 years later.[20] By contrast, a Bureau of Justice Statistics study that tracked more than a quarter million released prisoners for 3 years found a recidivism rate for released drug offenders of 67 percent.[21]

In 2004, to obtain more indepth understanding about the effectiveness of drug courts, NIJ launched a multisite, longitudinal study of their impact.[22] What precisely makes drug courts successful? Is it the type of offender accepted into the program or the type of treatment offered? What role does the judge's personality play? What are the costs and benefits? NIJ hopes to answer these and other questions as the research unfolds. Preliminary findings are anticipated in 2007.

Science in the courtroom

Scientific advances are changing the landscape of courtrooms. How prosecutors and defense attorneys use expert testimony and forensic evidence has changed dramatically during the last 10 years. Television shows that glamorize forensic investigation are highly popular (despite their inaccuracies in depicting how science helps solve crimes). Increasingly, court participants—judges, jurors, and attorneys alike—need to understand complex scientific evidence. But do recent advances in forensic science also advance justice?

As in other research areas, NIJ seeks solutions to these issues by drawing upon the expertise of scientists in relevant fields (e.g., forensic medicine) and by enhancing cooperation among these scientists and criminal justice professionals. Such cross-disciplinary cooperation helps NIJ identify pressing needs and develop more targeted research agendas.

[20] Roman, J., W. Townsend, and A. Singh Bhati, "Recidivism Rates for Drug Court Graduates: Nationally Based Estimates," final report to the National Institute of Justice, Washington, DC: The Urban Institute, July 2003 (NCJ 201229), available at http://www.ncjrs.org/pdffiles1/201229.pdf.

[21] Langan, P.A., and D.J. Levin, *Recidivism of Prisoners Released in 1994*, Washington, DC: U.S. Department of Justice, Bureau of Justice Statistics, June 2002 (NCJ 193427), available at http://www.ojp.usdoj.gov/bjs/pub/pdf/rpr94.pdf.

[22] The impact evaluation under way includes 29 drug court sites and 5 comparison sites. Interviews of more than 2,000 offenders will be conducted as they enter the court process (baseline), then again at 6 and 18 months. Recidivism will be examined 24 months after baseline. Researchers will evaluate the impact of various drug court strategies and conduct a cost-benefit analysis.

Of course, scientific tools cannot solve everything. That is why NIJ has brought together interagency working groups to examine how forensic science and technology can identify new ways to solve crime and ensure justice.

One technical working group is developing a guide to understanding how digital evidence must be presented in court.[23] Guides to investigating electronic crime scenes and forensic examination of digital evidence were published in 2001 and 2004, respectively (see "For more information," below).

NIJ plans and hosts national conferences and workshops with other forensic science, law enforcement, and criminal justice agencies and organizations. These Science and the Law conferences help practitioners understand the principles underlying scientific evidence.

In May 2004, NIJ hosted a summit attended by members of the American Academy of Forensic Sciences, the American Society of Crime Laboratory Directors, the International Association for Identification, and the National Association of Medical Examiners. The high-level discussion about policies and practices resulted in a report to Congress on the needs of forensic science service providers.[24]

For more information

- *Science and the Law: 2001 and 2002 National Conferences,* Special Report, Washington, DC: U.S. Department of Justice, National Institute of Justice, May 2004 (NCJ 202955), available at http://www.ncjrs.org/pdffiles1/nij/202955.pdf.

- *Forensic Examination of Digital Evidence: A Guide for Law Enforcement,* Special Report, Washington, DC: U.S. Department of Justice, National Institute of Justice, April 2004 (NCJ 199408), available at http://www.ncjrs.org/pdffiles1/nij/199408.pdf.

- *Electronic Crime Scene Investigation: A Guide for First Responders,* NIJ Guide, Washington, DC: U.S. Department of Justice, National Institute of Justice, July 2001 (NCJ 187736), available at http://www.ncjrs.org/pdffiles1/nij/187736.pdf.

23 *Digital Evidence in the Courtroom: A Guide for Law Enforcement and State and Local Prosecutors* is pending publication; three other guides related to electronic crime are in development.

24 The "180-Day Study Report: Status and Needs of United States Crime Laboratories," May 28, 2004, was prepared for the U.S. Senate Appropriations Committee by the American Society of Crime Laboratory Directors in collaboration with NIJ's Office of Science and Technology, the American Academy of Forensic Sciences, the International Association for Identification, and the National Association of Medical Examiners.

[25] Fromm, S., "Total Estimated Cost of Child Abuse and Neglect in the United States," *Cost-of-Injury Analysis,* National Clearinghouse on Child Abuse and Neglect Information, Administration for Children and Families, U.S. Department of Health and Human Services. Retrieved from the World Wide Web on January 27, 2005, http://nccanch. acf.hhs.gov/topics/prevention/develop/making/injury.cfm.

[26] Widom, C.S., and M.G. Maxfield, *An Update on the "Cycle of Violence,"* Research in Brief, Washington, DC: U.S. Department of Justice, National Institute of Justice, February 2001 (NCJ 184894), available at http://www.ncjrs. org/pdffiles1/nij/184894.pdf.

[27] *Violence Against Women: Identifying Risk Factors,* Research in Brief, Washington, DC: U.S. Department of Justice, National Institute of Justice, November 2004 (NCJ 197019), available at http://www.ncjrs.org/pdffiles1/ nij/197019.pdf.

[28] Finkelhor, D., and R. Ormrod, "Child Abuse Reported to the Police," *Juvenile Justice Bulletin,* Washington, DC: U.S. Department of Justice, Office of Juvenile Justice and Delinquency Prevention, May 2001 (NCJ 187238), available at http://www.ncjrs.org/pdffiles1/ojjdp/187238.pdf. See also Snyder, H.N., "Sexual Assault of Young Children as Reported to Law Enforcement: Victim, Incident, and Offender Characteristics," Washington, DC: U.S. Department of Justice, Bureau of Justice Statistics, July 2000 (NCJ 182990), available at http://www.ojp.usdoj.gov/bjs/pub/pdf/saycrle.pdf.

[29] Kilpatrick, D.G., B.E. Saunders, and D.W. Smith, *Youth Victimization: Prevalence and Implications,* Research in Brief, Washington, DC: U.S. Department of Justice, National Institute of Justice, April 2003 (NCJ 194972), available at http://www.ncjrs.org/pdffiles1/nij/194972.pdf.

[30] The success of child advocacy centers has not been empirically tested. A formal interview of child advocacy center directors and an extensive literature search found only one published outcome evaluation [Jenson, J.M., M. Jacobson, Y. Unrau, and R.L. Robinson, "Intervention for Victims of Child Sexual Abuse: An Evaluation of the Children's Advocacy Model," *Child and Adolescent Social Work Journal* 13(2) (1996):139–156]. The Office of Juvenile Justice and Delinquency Prevention is sponsoring a national evaluation of child advocacy centers, under way at the Crimes Against Children Research Center, University of New Hampshire.

Protecting child victims

Arguably the most vulnerable of all victims are children who have been abused or maltreated. The human pain and loss from child abuse and neglect are incalculable, but an analysis of the financial cost is estimated conservatively at $94 billion annually.[25] The long-range impact for criminal justice is striking: Children who have been abused and neglected are more likely than those who were not to become involved in criminal behavior later in life.[26] They are also more likely to be victimized as adults.[27]

From police records of child abuse, research indicates that family members and caretakers are responsible for 27 percent of the abuse, noncaretaker acquaintances are responsible for 63 percent, and strangers for 10 percent.[28] Research also confirms that for adolescents, much of the violence they experience is perpetrated by peers or someone they know well, and most of the sexual assaults (86 percent) and physical assaults (65 percent) they experience go unreported.[29]

During 2004, NIJ published a manual to help administrators of child advocacy centers evaluate the effects of their programs. Child advocacy centers serve abused children through a comprehensive approach to services for victims and their families. They stress coordination of investigation and intervention services by bringing together professionals and agencies in multidisciplinary teams. The goal is to ensure that children are not revictimized by the very system designed to protect them.[30]

The manual gives child advocacy center administrators the tools and knowledge they need to evaluate whether their center is achieving the standards established by the National Children's Alliance (NCA)—a child-friendly facility, a multidisciplinary team, child investigative interviews, a medical examination, mental health services, victim advocacy, and case review. To reduce the system-induced trauma children experience as a result of an investigation, NCA recommends limiting the number of interviews to which children are exposed.

For more information

- Jackson, S.L., *A Resource for Evaluating Child Advocacy Centers*, Special Report, Washington, DC: U.S. Department of Justice, National Institute of Justice, July 2004 (NCJ 192825), available at http://www.ncjrs.org/pdffiles1/nij/192825.pdf.

- Kilpatrick, D.G., B.E. Saunders, and D.W. Smith, *Youth Victimization: Prevalence and Implications*, Research in Brief, Washington, DC: U.S. Department of Justice, National Institute of Justice, April 2003 (NCJ 194972), available at http://www.ncjrs.org/pdffiles1/nij/194972.pdf.

Improving Corrections

As part of its mission to make prisons safer, NIJ sponsors research, development, and evaluation initiatives designed to anticipate and preempt, as well as mitigate, problems faced by corrections officers and administrators. Three of these initiatives are described here.

Keeping correctional officers safe

NIJ supports the development of performance standards for traditional law enforcement and corrections equipment, such as handcuffs, body armor, and metal detectors. One example of NIJ's work in this area was an assessment of personal alarm systems for correctional officers to use in an emergency. The study was conducted as a joint venture with the U.S. Department of Defense—specifically, the Information Technology Center of the U.S. Navy's Space and Naval Warfare Systems Command (SPAWAR).

Personal alarm systems rapidly distribute an alert from one correctional officer to another or to the facility's central command. Vendors are working on new systems using emerging technologies such as global positioning systems, biometrics, ultra wideband transmissions, and implanted microchips. SPAWAR produced a comprehensive guide to officer duress systems to help administrators identify their needs, select the appropriate system, and deploy it effectively. The guide also provides a scheme for classifying officer duress systems, a simplified duress system model, basic issues to consider during the selection process, a preview of current and emerging technologies, and an overview of products currently available.

For more information

- *Duress Systems in Corrections Facilities,* In Short—Toward Criminal Justice Solutions, Washington, DC: U.S. Department of Justice, National Institute of Justice, September 2004 (NCJ 205836), is available at http://www.ncjrs.org/pdffiles1/nij/205836.pdf. A highly detailed guide is the *Correctional Officer Duress Systems: Selection Guide,* Charleston, SC: SPAWAR Systems Charleston, October 2003 (NCJ 202947), available at http://www.ncjrs.org/pdffiles1/nij/grants/202947.pdf.

Understanding and reducing sexual assault in prisons

Sexual assault among prisoners is not well understood. The Prison Rape Elimination Act of 2003 calls for: (1) establishing national standards to detect and prevent sexual violence in prisons; (2) increasing the availability of data and related information in order to improve the management and administration of correctional facilities; and (3) increasing accountability for prisoner protection.

NIJ's immediate research agenda is to build knowledge about the incidence and prevalence of prison sexual violence, the investigation and prosecution of perpetrators, and the impact of sexual victimization in prison, including prevalence of sexually transmitted diseases among prison populations.

NIJ is currently leading a national qualitative study of sexual violence and prison culture that will be completed in late 2005. In 2004, NIJ made several awards related to prison sexual violence. Two studies are focusing on the development of risk assessment instruments to assist corrections practitioners in identifying likely victims and offenders. Two other NIJ grantees are conducting surveys to identify and characterize existing programs or practices designed to prevent sexual assault in adult and juvenile correctional facilities. The studies are mainly for information gathering, but researchers will make some preliminary assessments concerning promising programs or practices.

NIJ plans to award grants in 2005 for research on the impact of sexual violence on corrections and on the investigation and prosecution of sexual assault cases.

For more information

- *Data Collections for the Prison Rape Elimination Act of 2003,* Washington, DC: U.S. Department of Justice, Bureau of Justice Statistics, June 30, 2004 (NCJ 206109), available at http://www.ojp.usdoj.gov/bjs/pub/pdf/dcprea03.pdf.

A testimonial

Officers Chris Athen, Mike Bashor, Jeremy Branham, and Kevin Johnson of the Nevada Department of Corrections Special Response Team participated in two scenarios at last year's event. Last year the team drove all the way to Moundsville, but this year, most were able to fly.

"We got a grant to buy our plane tickets and raised money to pay for the rest of the trip," Branham said, adding that the team washed cars— and even dogs—to raise the money. "If it was dirty, we washed it," he said. Meanwhile, two team members drove their equipment more than 40 hours to be a part of the program. Johnson said the team was so impressed with the event last year that they knew they had to return.

Mock Prison Riot™

Every year NIJ's Office of Science and Technology's National Law Enforcement and Corrections Technology Center (NLECTC) and the Office of Law Enforcement Technology Commercialization (OLETC) sponsor a 4-day Mock Prison Riot™ at a former penitentiary in Moundsville, West Virginia. Police cadets and students play the role of prisoners staging an uprising so that law enforcement and corrections officers can train in realistic scenarios and test new less-lethal tools for controlling unruly crowds.

The event also allows administrators to consider the vulnerability of their facilities and assess such equipment as communication systems and drug detection devices. Vendors showcase their newest technology advances. Medical, fire, and emergency response personnel play support roles treating and evacuating staged injuries. Also present are many observers from Federal, State, and international corrections and law enforcement agencies; public and private organizations; and the media.

The Mock Prison Riot™ is in its seventh year, and its popularity continues to grow. The first year had 70 attendees. In May 2004, more than 1,300 persons attended from 41 States, Canada, Germany, Israel, and the United Kingdom. Riot scenarios included hostage situations, a hazardous materials spill, cell extractions, large-scale disturbances in the prison yard, possession of home-made weapons, and escape attempts.

For more information

• OLETC maintains a Mock Prison Riot™ Web site at http://www.oletc.org/riot; or contact the Office of Law Enforcement Technology Commercialization, 2001 Main Street, Wheeling, WV 26003; 888–306–5382 (toll-free).

Increasing Community Safety

Put in the simplest terms, all of NIJ's research programs and projects are geared to making lives safer and communities better places to live. For example, NIJ's support for studies to better understand criminal behavior led to groundbreaking strategies for prosecuting career criminals and guidelines for making pretrial release decisions that are modeled after research.

In 2004, NIJ supported research that directly or indirectly improves safety for citizens and law enforcement personnel—from risk assessments for battered women to police interventions that address gang and gun violence, from cutting-edge scanners for screening at schools and other public places to body armor standards. Some of these programs are described below.

Saving women's lives

Between 40 and 51 percent of women who are murdered in the United States are murdered by their husband or intimate partner.[31] In contrast, approximately 6 percent of men murdered are killed by their intimate partners.[32]

In the mid-1990's, NIJ began building a portfolio of research on violence against women designed to save women's lives by increasing knowledge and understanding of intimate partner homicide. Much of this research was conducted in conjunction with the U.S. Department of Justice's Office on Violence Against Women.

In November 2003, a special issue of the *NIJ Journal* was devoted exclusively to studies on this subject (see "For more information," page 26). That issue became one of the most frequently requested NIJ publications in 2004. Articles include descriptions of NIJ-funded research that found that women are most vulnerable immediately after they leave a relationship and are more likely to be murdered if they have been severely attacked by their intimate partner, especially if the attacks have escalated in severity. The research also shows that men who murder their intimate partners are more likely to use alcohol heavily and to use drugs. Gun ownership is also a risk factor.

[31] Brook, K., "When Men Murder Women: An Analysis of 2002 Homicide Data," Washington, DC: Violence Policy Center, September 2004, available at http://www.vpc.org/studies/wmmw2004.pdf.

[32] Fox, J.A., and M.W. Zawitz, *Homicide Trends in the U.S.,* "Trends by Gender," see statistical table, "Victim-Offender Relationship by Victim Gender, 1976–2002," Washington, DC: U.S. Department of Justice, Bureau of Justice Statistics, updated September 2004, available at http://www.ojp.usdoj.gov/bjs/homicide/gender.htm.

Most women who are murdered by their intimate partners have experienced one or more of several risk factors, such as being choked. Identifying which battering cases are most likely to lead to further injury could help women, their advocates, and the courts take protective action. Many criminal justice agencies use formal mechanisms such as checklists and assessment questionnaires to identify these high-risk cases. But how accurate are the assessment instruments? Can they really predict future harm?

To evaluate the accuracy of risk assessment tools, in 2000 NIJ initiated a study of four commonly used assessment instruments. Researchers at Johns Hopkins University completed the study in 2004. One instrument, the Danger Assessment Scale, appeared to be the most accurate.[33]

About half the time, abused women's perceptions that they are at high risk for additional violence are accurate. The rest of the time, they underestimate the threat of lethality or diminish the severity of the violence being perpetrated against them.[34] Thus, the researchers concluded that although victims' perceptions were important predictors of risk of reassault, they were not good enough to rely upon. Systematic risk assessment proved more reliable.

The women in the study told the researchers that the process of completing the risk assessment was "an eye-opening experience," leading them to take action to protect themselves from further abuse. This suggests the need for future research on whether risk assessments increase victims' self-protective actions.

For more information

- Campbell, J.C., D. Webster, J. Koziol-McLain, C.R. Block, D.W. Campbell, F. Gary, J.M. McFarlane, C.J. Sachs, P.W. Sharps, Y. Ulrich, S.A. Wilt, J. Manganello, X. Xu, J. Schollenberger, and V. Frye, "Assessing Risk Factors for Intimate Partner Homicide," *NIJ Journal* 250 (November 2003): 14–19, available at http://www.ncjrs.org/pdffiles1/jr000250e.pdf.

[33] Researchers assessed the accuracy of four instruments by administering them randomly to 1,307 battered women who sought help against a violent partner in various ways—calling 911, filing for a protective order, going to a shelter or hospital emergency room, or seeking domestic violence services at New York's Safe Horizon community offices. Six months later, participants were queried about all forms of abuse and violations of court orders since the risk assessment. They were also asked about protective measures and offender sanctions. Criminal records were checked 1 year after the baseline interview. The researchers' final report to the National Institute of Justice will be released through the National Criminal Justice Reference Service in 2005.

[34] Campbell, J.C., D. Webster, J. Koziol-McLain, C.R. Block, D.W. Campbell, F. Gary, J.M. McFarlane, C.J. Sachs, P.W. Sharps, Y. Ulrich, S.A. Wilt, J. Manganello, X. Xu, J. Schollenberger, and V. Frye, "Assessing Risk Factors for Intimate Partner Homicide," *NIJ Journal* 250 (November 2003): 16.

What is action research?

Action research occurs when researchers and their practitioner partners use data to develop strategies to solve local crime problems. To address an urgent problem—such as gang violence within a particular neighborhood— the researchers take a lead role in collecting and analyzing data to understand the patterns of the crime problem and potential sources. They remain actively involved during program implementation, provide feedback to implementers to refine and improve interventions, and ultimately determine how well the program achieved its goals.

35 For information about a prominent source that assembles research evidence, see Petrosino, A., D.P. Farrington, and L. Sherman, "The Campbell Collaboration: Helping to Understand 'What Works,'" *NIJ Journal* 251 (July 2004): 14–17, available at http://ncjrs.org/pdffiles1/jr000251d.pdf.

36 A rigorous evaluation found that the Boston project was associated with a 63-percent decrease in youth homicides per month, a 32-percent decrease in shots-fired calls for service per month, a 25-percent decrease in gun assaults per month, and a 44-percent decrease in the number of youth gun assaults per month in the highest risk district (Roxbury). See Kennedy, D.M., A.A. Braga, A.M. Piehl, and E.J. Waring, *Reducing Gun Violence: The Boston Gun Project's Operation Ceasefire,* Research Report, Washington, DC: U.S. Department of Justice, National Institute of Justice, September 2001 (NCJ 188741), available at http://www.ncjrs.org/pdffiles1/nij/188741.pdf.

37 Ibid., see exhibit 2–2, p. 58.

• Campbell, J.C., D. Webster, J. Koziol-McLain, C.R. Block, D.W. Campbell, M.A. Curry, F. Gary, J.M. McFarlane, C.J. Sachs, P.W. Sharps, Y. Ulrich, S.A. Wilt, J. Manganello, X. Xu, J. Schollenberger, V. Frye, and K. Laughon, "Risk Factors for Femicide in Abusive Relationships: Results From a Multisite Case Control Study," *American Journal of Public Health*, 93(7) (2003): 1089–1097.

Making neighborhoods safer

After several decades of helping law enforcement agencies develop better community crime prevention, NIJ is now leading the way toward evidence-based policies and practices.[35] The agency is reaching out to help cities develop focused problem-solving strategies based on best practices identified by research. This promotes researcher-practitioner partnerships to address problems at the local level.

Project Safe Neighborhoods, a national initiative involving NIJ and other U.S. Department of Justice agencies, builds on findings from action research that NIJ has been conducting since the mid-1990's. Projects in NIJ's action-research portfolio used data to pinpoint the exact nature of the problem, developed a strategic plan to address the problem, implemented the strategic plan, and then adjusted the strategy as needed.

Action research to reduce gun violence. One of NIJ's most successful action-research projects took place in Boston, Massachusetts, between 1995 and 1998. Called Operation Ceasefire, the Boston project dramatically reduced juvenile and youth homicides—by 63 percent overall.[36] For several months during the 2-year period of the study, youth homicides in Boston fell to zero.[37]

Other problem-solving projects sponsored by NIJ have experimented with approaches to reducing gun violence. In Indianapolis, Indiana, for example, researchers compared two strategies: (1) police stopping cars at random and confiscating illegal guns, and (2) police stopping only suspicious cars. The first strategy resulted in a higher number of confiscated guns, but the second strategy resulted in much lower gun crime. Even though police confiscated fewer guns during the second strategy, gun crime went down. The lesson from

Edmund F. McGarrell
Director, School of Criminal Justice,
Michigan State University

"[A]ction-research partnerships linking practitioners and researchers in problem-solving efforts ... are changing practice and making communities safer, while at the same time generating a new understanding of crime and criminal justice. NIJ deserves much credit as the catalyst for these partnerships."

Indianapolis: Police can reduce gun crime when they take away guns from the "right" people—potential criminals—and deter them from carrying guns.

Another problem-solving initiative sponsored by NIJ was the St. Louis (Missouri) Consent-to-Search Program, whereby police sought parental permission to search and seize guns from juveniles in their homes. The impact on gun crime was not as clear cut as the Indianapolis experience due to changes in the police department and resulting changes in program implementation. But one of the main lessons from St. Louis is that novel problem-solving approaches (police asking parents to allow the police to search their child's room) can work.

Project Safe Neighborhoods. Launched in 2001, Project Safe Neighborhoods (PSN) addresses gun violence by forming or strengthening strategic partnerships among Federal, State, and local agencies, under the auspices of the local United States Attorney. The five core elements of PSN are:

- Partnerships that include local, tribal, State, and Federal law enforcement; local, State, and Federal prosecutors; probation and parole officials; researchers; and community groups, such as faith-based organizations.

- Strategic planning through collection and analysis of data to identify the precise nature of the gun crime problem.

- Training for all participants.

- Outreach to involve the community and to let potential offenders know that they will "do hard time for gun crime."

- Accountability that defines success through actual outcome data.

Because each jurisdiction is unique, PSN partners tailor these elements to suit the particular needs in their district.

In 2004, NIJ staff and grantees provided technical assistance and research support to all 94 Project Safe Neighborhood sites. Training was designed to help PSN partners develop strategic problem-solving approaches to address endemic local gun crime problems. In addition, the NIJ-funded research grantees will conduct case studies of promising intervention strategies and comprehensive case studies assessing the implementation and impacts of PSN in selected sites.

For more information

- Kennedy, D.M., A.A. Braga, A.M. Piehl, and E.J. Waring, *Reducing Gun Violence: The Boston Gun Project's Operation Ceasefire*, Research Report, Washington, DC: U.S. Department of Justice, National Institute of Justice, September 2001 (NCJ 188741), available at http://www.ncjrs.org/pdffiles1/nij/188741.pdf.

- McGarrell, E.F., S. Chermak, and A. Weiss, *Reducing Gun Violence: Evaluation of the Indianapolis Police Department's Directed Patrol Project*, Research Report, Washington, DC: U.S. Department of Justice, National Institute of Justice, November 2002 (NCJ 188740), available at http://www.ncjrs.org/pdffiles1/nij/188740.pdf.

- Decker, S., and R. Rosenfeld, *Reducing Gun Violence: The St. Louis Consent-to-Search Program*, Research Report, Washington, DC: U.S. Department of Justice, National Institute of Justice, November 2004 (NCJ 191332), available at http://www.ncjrs.org/pdffiles1/nij/191332.pdf.

- Project Safe Neighborhoods Web site at http://www.psn.gov.

Technology testing and evaluation

NIJ's Office of Science and Technology oversees research and development of new technology and technical standards to improve the safety of citizens, communities, and law enforcement personnel. Several projects in 2004 showed significant promise for easier, more effective detection of illegal weapons or entry.

Making schools safer. As part of NIJ's research and development agenda to make schools safer, NIJ worked with the New York City Police Department's

School Safety Division to test a walk-through weapons detection portal in a Manhattan high school. The portal, called "Secure Scan 2000," uses new magnetometer technology to "see" very small metal objects (such as razor blades, which were being used in gang-based slashings at the school).[38] In 2004, demonstration of an improved version of the portal at a Bronx, New York, high school reduced the level of false or nuisance alarms by 30 percent and the number of slashings by half. The research, development, and testing of this new portal for schools could lead to major improvements in the metal detector portals currently used in most airports and courthouses.

Other technology tested as part of NIJ's safe schools initiative is also expected to have wider application. In three New Jersey schools, for example, NIJ installed and evaluated a system that has improved the school's ability to ensure that the person picking up a student is authorized to do so. The system uses the iris of a person's eye for identification. During 9,400 iris scannings at the schools, there were no known false positives or other misidentifications. The system made accurate identifications and unlocked the door 78 percent of the time. Failures that occurred were due to problems with lighting (especially on sunny days), with someone improperly lining up with the scanner (16 percent of failures), or with persons who were not enrolled in the program using the scanner (6 percent of failures).

Making lives safer with biometrics. For several years, NIJ has been expanding understanding of biometric technology and exploring how to use it to improve public safety. Biometric technologies that scan or measure unique physical characteristics (such as the iris scan experiment) are more reliable than traditional identifiers such as drivers' licenses and identification or swipe cards. Because the systems are computer-based, they can provide records that other methods cannot. But more importantly, biometrics requires no user name, password, or series of numbers to confirm identity.

[38] Secure Scan 2000 was developed by the U.S. Department of Energy's Idaho National Engineering and Environmental Laboratory, with funding provided by NIJ.

NIJ also plays a lead role in research and development concerning finger imaging and face recognition technology. In 2004, for example, NIJ evaluated 13 fingerprint identification algorithms in response to a requirement of the Patriot Act to evaluate the FBI's Integrated Automated Fingerprint Identification System (IAFIS), which contains fingerprint records for more than 47 million subjects.

NIJ participates in several joint biometric efforts, including the U.S. Department of Justice's Biometrics Cooperative and the government-wide International Committee for Information Technology Standards, which has issued three biometrics standards: iris image, finger image, and face recognition formats for data interchange.

For more information

- "Cause for Alarm," *TechBeat,* Winter 2003: 2–3, available at http://www.nlectc. org/techbeat/winter2003/SafeSchWint03.pdf.

- Biometrics catalog at http://www.biometricscatalog.org.

- On the Integrated Automated Fingerprint Identification System, see http://www. fbi.gov/hq/cjisd/iafis.htm.

Appendixes

'04

Appendix A
Financial Data

Exhibit 1: Trends in NIJ's Research and Development Portfolio, FY 1995–2004

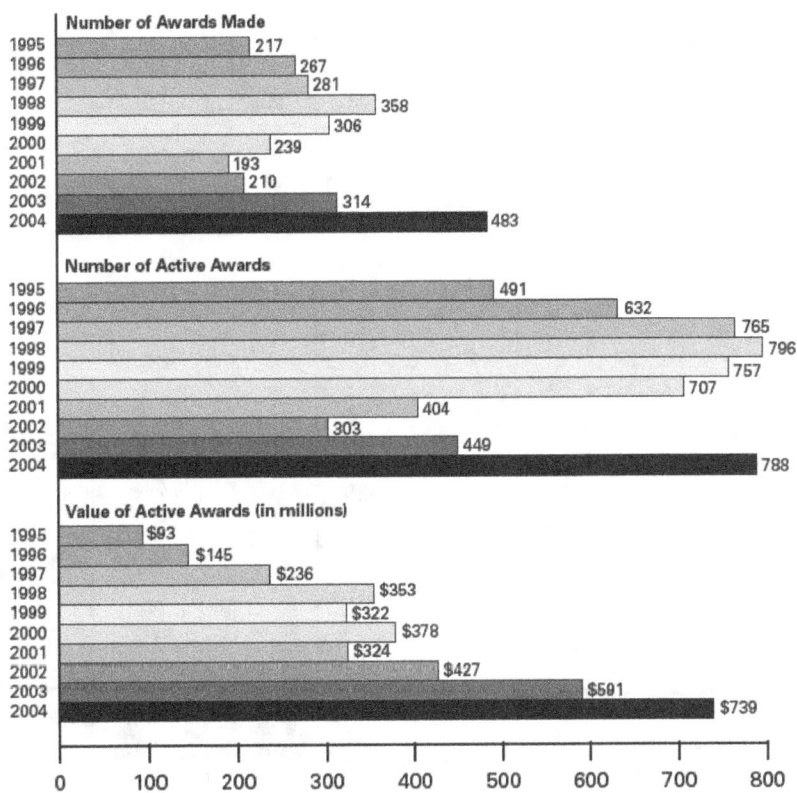

Number of Awards Made

Year	Value
1995	217
1996	267
1997	281
1998	358
1999	306
2000	239
2001	193
2002	210
2003	314
2004	483

Number of Active Awards

Year	Value
1995	491
1996	632
1997	765
1998	796
1999	757
2000	707
2001	404
2002	303
2003	449
2004	788

Value of Active Awards (in millions)

Year	Value
1995	$93
1996	$145
1997	$236
1998	$353
1999	$322
2000	$378
2001	$324
2002	$427
2003	$591
2004	$739

0   100   200   300   400   500   600   700   800

Exhibit 2: Sources of NIJ Funds, in Millions, FY 1995–2004

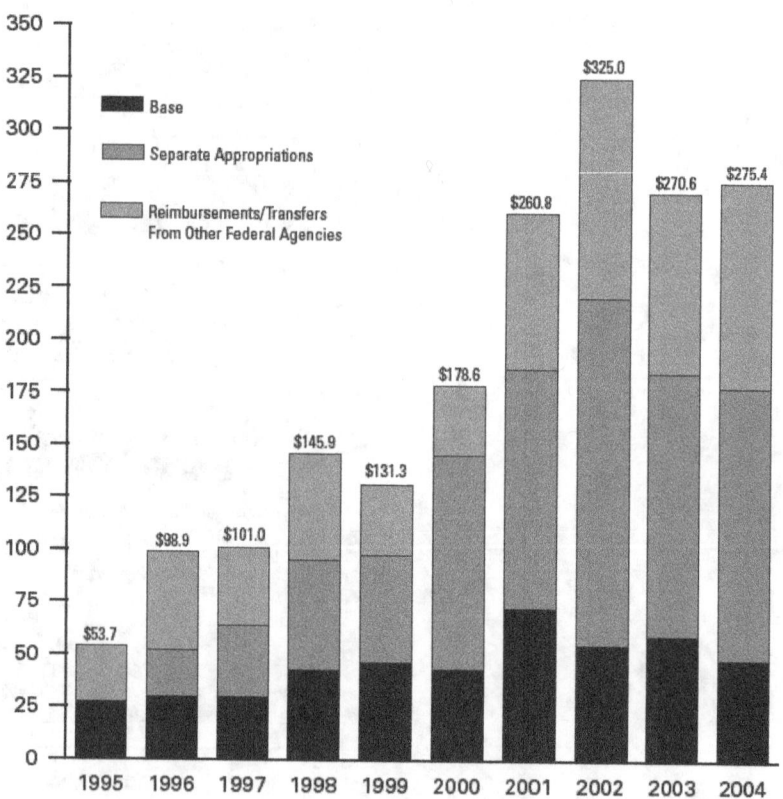

Exhibit 3: Allocation of NIJ Funds as a Percentage of Total Expenditures,*
FY 2004

Social Science		
	Research	11%
	Evaluation	4%
Science and Technology		
	Capacity Building**	45%
	Research and Development	18%
	Technology Assistance	11%
	Standards	4%
Program Support		3%
Dissemination		2%
Other		2%

*Total expenditures of $275.4 million include NIJ's base appropriation of $48 million plus separate
appropriations and funds transferred from other agencies.

**Grants to improve and enhance crime labs.

Appendix B

NIJ Awards in FY 2004 (includes first-time awards and supplements to previous awards)

ADMINISTRATIVE SUPPORT

Audit Services for U.S. Crime Laboratories Performing DNA Analysis
National Forensic Science Technology Center
2004–DN–BX–0079
$1,000,000

Meeting and Editorial Support
Aspen Systems Corporation
1996–MU–MU–K011
$61,000

NIJ Surplus Property Program
Ultimate Enterprises, Ltd.
1996–LB–VX–K002
$123,000

COMMUNICATION AND
INFORMATION TECHNOLOGIES

Advanced Development and Testing of the Voice Response Translator
Integrated Wave Technologies
2004–IJ–CX–K042
$99,983

California Integrated Laboratory Information Management System
California Department of Justice
2004–LP–CX–0010
$1,987,000

Capital Wireless Integrated Network
University of Maryland
2001–RB–CX–K001
$223,891

Center for Criminal Justice Technology Information Systems Integration Projects
Mitretek Systems, Inc.
2001–LT–BX–K002
$3,268,432

CommTech Program Support: Kansas City Regional Crime Analysis
University of Denver
2001–RD–CX–K001
$49,637

Comprehensive Suite of New Technology Standards for Interoperable Communications Networks for Land Mobile Communications
APCO Automated Frequency Coordination
1997–LB–VX–K002
$200,000

Criminal Justice Information System, 2004
South Carolina Law Enforcement Division
2004–RG–CX–K009
$1,484,216

Development of a Law Enforcement Technology Wireless Data/Communication Infrastructure
Center for Rural Development
2003–RD–CX–K010
$1,978,955

Development of a Speech-to-Forms Translator for Border Agencies
Language Systems, Inc.
2004–IJ–CX–K053
$49,908

Impact of Information Security in Academic Institutions on Safety and Security
Columbia University Teachers College
2004–IJ–CX–0045
$205,876

Implementation of Accelerated Information Sharing for Law Enforcement
National Law Enforcement Telecommunication System, Inc.
2002–MU–MU–K005
$844,855

Interoperable Voice Communication and Information Sharing: Research and Development
Aerospace Corporation
2004–IJ–CX–K028
$135,000

Interoperable Voice Communication and Information Sharing: Research and Development
Center for Advanced Public Safety Information Technologies
2004–IJ–CX–K029
$518,093

Interoperable Voice Communication and Information Sharing: Research and Development
State University of New York
2004–LT–BX–K027
$161,716

Interoperable Voice Communication and Information Sharing: Research and Development
University of Central Florida
2004–IJ–CX–K030
$293,768

Lowcountry Information Technology Improvement Project, Phase III
South Carolina Research Authority
2002–MU–MU–K011
$2,473,694

National Criminal Intelligence Information Sharing
Automated Regional Justice Information System
2004–RG–CX–K018
$375,000

Public Safety Interoperability Communications Resource, Phase II: Evaluation and Assessment Guidance for Law Enforcement and Security Technology Supplement
Eastern Kentucky University
2003–IJ–CX–K102
$1,150,000

Redesign of Alaska Public Safety Information Network
Alaska Department of Public Safety
2004–RG–CX–K007
$2,473,694

Responsive Efforts to Ensure Integral Needs in Staffing
Association of Public Safety Communications Officials, Inc.
2003–MU–MU–K103
$200,000

Software-Defined Radio Project, Phase II
South Carolina Research Authority
2002–MU–MU–K011
$2,253,040

State Communications Initiative, Phase IV
South Carolina Research Authority
2002–MU–MU–K011
$989,450

State Leadership in Public Safety Wireless Interoperability
National Governors Association, Center for Best Practices
2002–RG–CX–K001
$50,000

Support Services for NIJ's Interoperability/ AGILE Program
Center for Technology Commercialization
2001–LT–BX–K011
$99,943

Technological Interoperability
Albany, City of
2004–LT–BX–K005
$395,791

Wireless Accelerated Response Network: Wireless Broadband Citywide Network for First Responders
District of Columbia
2004–MU–MU–K096
$398,200

XML Standards for Integrated Justice
Georgia Tech Applied Research Corporation
2003–IJ–CX–K030
$400,000

COMMUNITY JUSTICE

Community Organizations and Crime: Examining the Social-Institutional Processes of Neighborhoods
Urban Institute
2004–IJ–CX–0049
$198,757

Graduate Research Fellowship: Contextual Effects on Juvenile Delinquency— Modeling Differential Effects of School and Neighborhood Social Organization
University of Chicago
2004–IJ–CX–0012
$20,000

COMPUTER CRIME

Chicago Internet Experiment
University of Illinois
2004–IJ–CX–0021
$298,644

College-Level Academic Program for Electronic Crime and Digital Forensics at Champlain College
Champlain College, Inc.
2004–MU–MU–K001
$185,000

Consensus Gathering for Certification for Digital Evidence Professionals
University of Central Florida
1998–IJ–CX–K003
$79,997

Support Services for NIJ's Electronic Crime Program
Center for Technology Commercialization
2001–LT–BX–K011
$25,000

CORRECTIONS

Addressing Prison Sexual Violence
Urban Institute
2004–RP–BX–0001
$400,000

Aftercare Services for Juvenile Parolees with Mental Disorders
Children's Research Institute
2004–IJ–CX–0084
$299,652

Assessment of Risk Factors Associated With Sexual Violence in the Texas Prison System
The Institute
2004–RP–BX–0003
$183,378

Correctional Industries Preparing Inmates for Reentry: Recidivism and Postrelease Employment Evaluation
University of Baltimore
2004–DD–BX–1001
$200,000

Intersection of Prisons and Child Welfare: Findings From a Multi-State Collaboration
University of California
2004–IJ–CX–0036
$100,000

Pennsylvania Task Force on Prison Overcrowding
County Commissioners Association of Pennsylvania
2004–IJ–CX–0007
$347,725

Prison Population Computer Simulation Model Project
Alabama Sentencing Commission
2004–DD–BX–1014
$98,948

Recidivism Among Female Prisoners
California State University—Fresno
2004–IJ–CX–0038
$35,000

Research on Prison Sexual Violence
Colorado Division of Criminal Justice
2004–RP–BX–0095
$451,251

Risk Markers for Sexual Vulnerability and Violence in Prison: Development of a Risk Classification System for Inmates
University of Virginia
2004–RP–BX–0004
$397,647

Working With Technology in Corrections
American Correctional Association
1996–LB–VX–K004
$199,836

COURTS

Courtroom of the 21st Century
College of William and Mary
2004–DD–BX–K011
$494,739

Development of Alternative Modalities for Providing DNA Training for the Nation's Prosecutors
American Prosecutors Research Institute
2004–DN–BX–K017
$400,000

Drug Court Evaluation Plan Review and Technical Assistance Initiative
National Association of Drug Court Professionals
2004–DC–BX–K005
$195,727

Feasibility and Efficacy of Performance Measures in Prosecution and Their Application to Community Prosecution
American Prosecutors Research Institute
2004–PP–CX–0002
$385,000

John Doe Indictment Project
New York, City of
2004–RC–CX–K014
$347,725

Visiting Fellowship Program: Multi-State Analysis of Time Consumption in Capital Appeals
City University of New York
2004–IJ–CX–0005
$85,530

CRIME LAB IMPROVEMENT

Crime Laboratory Improvement Program
Allegheny County Forensic Lab, Division of the Coroner's Office
2004–LP–CX–K015
$248,375

Crime Laboratory Improvement Program
Baltimore, City of
2004–LP–CX–K033
$993,005

Crime Laboratory Improvement Program
King County Sheriff's Office
2004–RG–CX–K011
$248,375

Crime Laboratory Improvement Program
Maryland State Police
2004–LP–CX–K032
$820,273

Crime Laboratory Improvement Program
New Jersey Department of Law and Public Safety
2004–LP–CX–K020
$1,987,000

Crime Laboratory Improvement Program
Northern Illinois Police Crime Laboratory
2004–LP–CX–K010
$496,750

Crime Laboratory Improvement Program
Williamson, County of
2004–RC–CX–K021
$29,805

DNA Equipment Project
Indiana State Police
2004–LP–CX–K006
$496,750

DNA Improvement
Indiana State Police
2004–LP–CX–K097
$1,490,250

Equipment Purchase for DNA Automation
Washoe County Sheriff's Office
2004–LT–BX–K009
$247,357

Establishment of a Forensic DNA Analysis Laboratory at North Dakota State University
North Dakota State University
2004–RG–CX–K001
$989,477

Expansion and Enhancement of the Southeast Missouri Regional Crime Lab
Southeast Missouri State University
2004–LP–CX–K049
$963,695

Forensic Crime Lab Improvement Program, 2003
South Carolina Law Enforcement Division
2004–LP–CX–K001
$2,483,750

Forensic DNA Analysis Capability— Crime Lab Improvement
Colorado Springs, City of
2004–RC–CX–K019
$496,750

Forensic Laboratory Improvement, 2004
South Carolina Law Enforcement Division
2003–IJ–CX–K022
$1,484,216

High-Tech Crime Lab System Improvement
South Carolina Law Enforcement Division
2003–IJ–CX–K022
$989,477

Indian Country Crime Lab Services in New Mexico
Albuquerque, City of
2004–RC–CX–K075
$1,308,755

Laboratory Enhancement
New York, City of
2004–LT–BX–K013
$993,500

Phoenix Police Department Crime Lab Improvement Program
Phoenix, City of
2004–LP–CX–0016
$993,500

Upgrade of Bureau of Criminal Identification and Investigation Laboratory Analytical Capabilities and Efficiency
Ohio Office of the Attorney General
2002–LP–CX–K007
$789,707

Virginia Forensic Laboratory Improvement Program, 2004
Virginia, Commonwealth of
2004–LP–CX–0001
$1,490,250

CRIME PREVENTION

Catching Stolen Vehicles: Additional Capabilities for a Mobile License Plate Reading System
Critical Response Manufacturing
2004–IJ–CX–K016
$198,226

Data Sharing and Geographic Information Technology: Implementation, Coordination, and Support for the East Valley Community's Mapping, Planning, and Analysis for Safety Strategies
Redlands, City of
2004–DD–BX–1190
$494,739

Graduate Fellowship: Deterrent Effect of Curfew Enforcement— Operation Night Watch in St. Louis
University of Missouri—St. Louis
2004–IJ–CX–0008
$20,000

Handheld Metal Detector Testing
Aspen Systems Corporation
1996–MU–MU–K011
$150,000

Multidimensional Treatment Foster Care with New York Girls: Outcomes and Transportability
Center for Research to Practice
2004–IJ–CX–0094
$100,000

Precision Indoor-Outdoor Personnel Location System II
Worcester Polytechnic Institute
2003–IJ–CX–K025
$148,422

Security Industry Scope and Emerging Trends
ASIS Foundation, Inc.
2004–IJ–CX–0033
$97,420

CRIMINAL JUSTICE RESEARCH

**Breaking the Cycle of Behavioral
Health Problems and Crime**
University of Connecticut Health Center
2004–DD–BX–1025
$940,000

**Campbell Collaboration Crime and Justice
Group Expedited Review Project**
University of Pennsylvania
2004–DD–BX–0003
$132,945

Center on Law and Security
New York University
2004–DD–BX–1012
$1,484,216

Committee on Law and Justice
National Academy of Sciences
2001–MU–MU–0007
$250,000

Creation of a Uniform Crime Reports Utility
Ohio State University
2004–IJ–CX–0083
$122,890

**Graduate Research Fellowship: Comparison
of Imputation Methodologies in the Offenses-
Known Uniform Crime Reports**
University of Illinois
2004–IJ–CX–0006
$19,997

**National Clearinghouse for Science,
Technology, and the Law**
Stetson University, Inc.
2003–IJ–CX–K024
$2,968,432

**W.E.B. DuBois Fellowship: Exploring the
Factors Influencing Family Members'
Connections to Incarcerated Individuals**
Rutgers—State University of New Jersey
2004–IJ–CX–0043
$78,767

DRUGS AND CRIME

**Chinese Connection: Changing Patterns of
Drug Trafficking in the Golden Triangle**
Rutgers—State University of New Jersey
2004–IJ–CX–0023
$199,995

**Context of Drug Markets: The
Direct and Indirect Influence of
Gender in Drug Market Activities**
Arizona State University
2004–IJ–CX–0014
$34,946

**Exploring the Drugs/Crime Connection
Within the Electronic Dance
and Hip-Hop Nightclub Scenes**
University of Delaware
2004–IJ–CX–0040
$283,563

EDUCATION AND TRAINING

**Advanced Distance Learning to
Enhance the Gathering, Preservation,
and Use of DNA Evidence**
Dartmouth College
2004–IJ–CX–K041
$1,697,343

**DNA Academies and Officers of the Court
CD–ROM Project Funding**
National Forensic Science Technology Center
2000–RC–CX–K001
$2,000,000

**Forensic Hair Examination Workshop
and Atlas Under the President's DNA
Initiative Funding**
West Virginia University
2001–RC–CX–K003
$340,000

**Marshall University Forensic
Science Center DNA Training**
Marshall University Research Corporation
2001–RC–CX–K002
$520,000

New Hampshire Distance Learning Project
New Hampshire Department of Justice
2004–DD–BX–K023
$989,477

**Scientific Working Group for Digital
Evidence and FBI ACES Forensic Computer
Training: Ongoing Support**
University of Central Florida
1998–IJ–CX–K003
$595,768

Testing and Evaluation of Technology-Based Delivery of Model Training Programs in DNA Continuing Education
National Forensic Science Technology Center
2000–RC–CX–K001
$1,978,955

Western Forensic and Law Enforcement Training Center
Western Forensic Law Enforcement Training Center at Colorado State University—Pueblo
2003–DD–BX–K013
$989,477

EVALUATION

Evaluation and Assessment Guidance for Law Enforcement and Security Technology Supplement
Eastern Kentucky University
2003–IJ–CX–K102
$424,628

Evaluation of a Comprehensive Approach to Reducing Gun Violence in Detroit
Michigan State University
2004–IJ–CX–0022
$243,461

Evaluation of Father Flanagan's Boys' Home (Girls and Boys Town)
Development Services Group, Inc.
2004–IJ–CX–0029
$559,998

Evaluations of Byrne Funded Projects, FY 2004
Abt Associates, Inc.
2004–DD–BX–1467
$671,092

Evaluations of Byrne Funded Projects, FY 2004
Institute for Law and Justice
2004–DD–BX–1466
$350,379

Multisite Evaluation of the Serious and Violent Offender Reentry Initiative, Phase II
RTI International
2004–RE–CX–0002
$10,127,061

FORENSICS, GENERAL

American Academy of Applied Forensics
Central Piedmont Community College
2001–RC–CX–K009
$794,800

Forensic Science Initiative
West Virginia University
2001–RC–CX–K003
$741,075

Marshall University Forensic Science Center and Forensic Resource Network Initiatives to Improve Forensic Crime Laboratories
Marshall University Research Corporation
2001–RC–CX–K002
$3,265,276

Northeast Regional Forensics Institute
State University of New York
2004–LP–CX–K025
$1,490,250

Status and Needs of the Forensic Digital Audio-Video Communities
University of Central Florida
1998–IJ–CX–K003
$67,616

Streamlining Physical Evidence Collection and Forensic Analysis
Florida Gulf Coast University
2004–LP–CX–K048
$1,241,875

West Virginia University Forensic Science Initiative, FY 2003
West Virginia University
2003–RC–CX–K001
$3,974,000

West Virginia University Forensic Science Initiative, FY 2004
West Virginia University
2001–RC–CX–K003
$3,957,910

Wildlife DNA Profiling and Forensics
East Stroudsburg University of Pennsylvania
2004–LP–CX–K012
$397,400

FORENSICS, RESEARCH AND DEVELOPMENT

Application of Laser-Induced Breakdown Spectroscopy to Forensic Science: Analysis of Glass Samples
University of Central Florida
2004–IJ–CX–K031
$210,728

Development of Microfluidic Devices for the Rapid Isolation and Detection of Drugs of Abuse
Florida International University
2004–WG–BX–K077
$499,865

Evaluation and Application of Polynomial Texture Mapping for Footwear and Tire Impression Evidence Comparisons
California Department of Justice
2004–IJ–CX–K008
$128,802

Forensic Glass Analysis by Laser Ablation Inductively Coupled Plasma Mass Spectrometry: Assessing the Feasibility of Correlating Windshield Composition and Supplier
Sacramento, County of
2004–IJ–CX–K007
$36,053

Internet Forensic Toolkit for Law Enforcement
University of California—San Diego
2004–MU–MU–K002
$180,000

Quantitative Assessment of the Discriminative Power of Handwriting
State University of New York
2004–IJ–CX–K050
$490,700

Statistical Methods for Estimating a Minimum Postmortem Interval: Evaluation Using Insect Growth Data
West Virginia University
2002–LT–BX–4001
$101,467

FORENSICS AND INVESTIGATIVE SCIENCES

DNA Capacity Enhancement Program Formula Grants

Alabama Department of Forensic Sciences
2004–DN–BX–K066
$404,856

Alameda, County of
2004–DN–BX–K068
$123,815

Alaska Department of Public Safety
2004–DN–BX–K063
$73,675

Albuquerque, City of
2004–DN–BX–K203
$168,485

Allegheny, County of
2004–DN–BX–K091
$84,594

Anne Arundel, County of
2004–DN–BX–K126
$72,224

Arizona Criminal Justice Commission
2004–DN–BX–K067
$376,622

Arizona Department of Public Safety
2004–DN–BX–K262
$236,238

Arkansas State Crime Laboratory
2004–DN–BX–K064
$233,618

Austin, City of
2004–DN–BX–K186
$121,866

Baltimore, City of
2004–DN–BX–K143
$180,218

Baltimore, County of
2004–DN–BX–K132
$135,092

Bexar, County of
2004–DN–BX–K191
$217,319

Boston, City of
2004–DN–BX–K127
$24,520

Broward Sheriff's Office
2004–DN–BX–K101
$199,539

California Department of Justice
2004–DN–BX–K065
$1,318,613

Charlotte, City of
2004–DN–BX–K188
$57,776

Colorado Department of Public Safety
2004–DN–BX–K100
$259,506

Columbus, City of
2004–DN–BX–K208
$150,542

Connecticut Department of Public Safety
2004–DN–BX–K104
$218,709

Contra Costa, County of
2004–DN–BX–K071
$139,068

Cuyahoga County Coroners Office
2004–DN–BX–K195
$62,322

Dallas, County of
2004–DN–BX–K187
$479,806

Delaware Health and Social Services
2004–DN–BX–K099
$98,233

Denver, City and County of
2004–DN–BX–K103
$63,103

Detroit Police Department
2004–DN–BX–K148
$419,825

District of Columbia Metropolitan Police
Department
2004–DN–BX–K102
$189,357

DuPage County Office of the Sheriff
2004–DN–BX–K122
$36,384

Erie, County of
2004–DN–BX–K196
$126,521

Florida Department of Law Enforcement
2004–DN–BX–K107
$1,697,495

Fresno County Sheriff's Department
2004–DN–BX–K079
$139,584

Georgia Bureau of Investigation
2004–DN–BX–K109
$797,707

Harris, County of
2004–DN–BX–K199
$195,799

Honolulu, City and County of
2004–DN–BX–K111
$71,286

Houston, City of
2004–DN–BX–K193
$487,014

Idaho State Police
2004–DN–BX–K106
$71,286

Illinois State Police
2004–DN–BX–K115
$1,529,577

Indiana State Police
2004–DN–BX–K123
$446,904

Iowa, State of
2004–DN–BX–K110
$170,384

Kansas Bureau of Investigation
2004–DN–BX–K116
$123,038

Kansas City Board of Police Commissioners
2004–DN–BX–K173
$149,439

Kentucky, Commonwealth of
2004–DN–BX–K125
$231,932

Kern, County of
2004–DN–BX–K076
$81,445

Lake, County of
2004–DN–BX–K211
$61,603

Las Vegas Metropolitan Police Department
2004–DN–BX–K204
$281,455

Los Angeles, City of
2004–DN–BX–K078
$527,799

Los Angeles, County of
2004–DN–BX–K073
$562,217

Louisiana State Police
2004–DN–BX–K124
$603,089

Maine Department of Public Safety
2004–DN–BX–K146
$71,286

Mansfield, City of
2004–DN–BX–K209
$49,610

Maryland State Police
2004–DN–BX–K145
$181,847

Massachusetts State Police
2004–DN–BX–K128
$607,962

Miami-Dade, County of
2004–DN–BX–K108
$535,895

Michigan, State of
2004–DN–BX–K165
$683,286

Minnesota, State of
2004–DN–BX–K166
$272,761

Mississippi Department of Public Safety
2004–DN–BX–K185
$200,244

Missouri Southern State University
2004–DN–BX–K178
$44,448

Missouri State Highway Patrol
2004–DN–BX–K181
$161,577

Montana Department of Justice
2004–DN–BX–K176
$71,286

Montgomery, County of
2004–DN–BX–K142
$98,875

Montgomery, County of
2004–DN–BX–K206
$219,333

Nebraska State Patrol
2004–DN–BX–K194
$110,258

New Hampshire Department of Safety,
Division of Motor Vehicles
2004–DN–BX–K207
$71,286

New Jersey Department of
Law and Public Safety
2004–DN–BX–K225
$495,973

New Mexico, State of
2004–DN–BX–K205
$110,187

New York State Division of
Criminal Justice Services
2004–DN–BX–K210
$1,803,811

North Carolina Department of
Crime Control and Public Safety
2004–DN–BX–K168
$736,823

North Dakota, State of
2004–DN–BX–K169
$71,286

Northern Illinois Police Crime Laboratory
2004–DN–BX–K120
$22,790

Oakland, City of
2004–DN–BX–K077
$82,727

Ohio Office of the Attorney General
2004–DN–BX–K202
$271,705

Oklahoma State Bureau of Investigation
2004–DN–BX–K183
$357,242

Orange, County of
2004–DN–BX–K069
$226,674

Oregon State Police
2004–DN–BX–K189
$209,182

Palm Beach County Sheriff's Office
2004–DN–BX–K105
$181,765

Pennsylvania State Police
2004–DN–BX–K097
$593,165

Philadelphia, City of
2004–DN–BX–K094
$329,313

Prince George's, County of
2004–DN–BX–K144
$185,189

Rhode Island Department of Health,
Division of Laboratories
2004–DN–BX–K190
$71,286

Richland County Government
2004–DN–BX–K192
$71,129

Sacramento, County of
2004–DN–BX–K082
$191,474

San Bernardino, County of
2004–DN–BX–K080
$201,238

San Diego, City of
2004–DN–BX–K081
$137,581

San Diego, County of
2004–DN–BX–K070
$151,953

San Francisco, City and County of
2004–DN–BX–K072
$120,285

San Mateo, County of
2004–DN–BX–K075
$52,372

Santa Clara, County of
2004–DN–BX–K083
$127,316

Sedgwick, County of
2004–DN–BX–K117
$84,742

South Carolina Law Enforcement Division
2004–DN–BX–K250
$614,654

South Dakota Office of the Attorney General
2004–DN–BX–K184
$71,286

Southeast Missouri State University
2004–DN–BX–K177
$34,151

St. Charles, County of
2004–DN–BX–K179
$44,505

St. Louis County Police
2004–DN–BX–K182
$95,641

St. Louis Metropolitan Police Department
2004–DN–BX–K180
$90,940

Tarrant, County of
2004–DN–BX–K201
$64,803

Texas, State of
2004–DN–BX–K198
$787,606

Union, County of
2004–DN–BX–0224
$157,451

University of North Texas Health
Science Center—Fort Worth
2004–DN–BX–K197
$205,575

Utah Department of Public Safety
2004–DN–BX–K200
$111,477

Ventura, County of
2004–DN–BX–K074
$48,798

Vermont Department of Public Safety
2004–DN–BX–K174
$71,286

Virginia, Commonwealth of
2004–DN–BX–K167
$431,770

Washington State Patrol
2004–DN–BX–K170
$425,839

West Virginia State Police
2004–DN–BX–K172
$85,741

Wisconsin Department of Justice
2004–DN–BX–K175
$248,589

Wyoming Office of the Attorney General
2004–DN–BX–K171
$71,286

DNA, Missing Persons

DNA Testing of Unidentified Remains
University of North Texas Health
Science Center—Fort Worth
2004–DN–BX–K212
$750,000

**Field Test of Current Technology
Used to Identify Human Remains**
University of North Texas Health
Science Center—Fort Worth
2004–DN–BX–K214
$249,902

**Focus Group: Using Technology to Assist in
the Identification of Human Remains**
University of Central Florida
1998–IJ–CX–K003
$186,892

**Standardized Sample Collection
Kit for Unidentified Remains and
Relatives of Missing Persons**
University of North Texas Health
Science Center—Fort Worth
2004–DN–BX–K213
$415,493

DNA, Research and Development

**Development and Validation of a
Standardized Canine STR Panel for
Use in Forensic Casework**
University of California
2004–DN–BX–K007
$310,798

**Development of an Automated System to
Detect Spermatozoa on Laboratory Slides**
Vermont Department of Public Safety
2004–DN–BX–K003
$214,629

**Forensic Stain Identification by
RT-PCR Analysis**
Vermont Department of Public Safety
2004–DN–BX–K002
$240,404

**Generating More Precise Postmortem Interval
Estimates With Entomological Evidence**
Michigan State University
2004–DN–BX–K005
$185,001

Graduate Research Fellowship: Bayesian Networks in Forensic Science
North Carolina State University
2004–DN–BX–K006
$20,000

A Hand-Held DNA-Based Forensic Tool
Cornell University
2004–DN–BX–K001
$644,251

Laser Microdissection Separation of Pure Spermatozoa Populations From Mixed Cell Samples for Forensic DNA Analysis
Rosalind Franklin University of
Medicine and Science
2004–DN–BX–K215
$449,829

Microfabricated Capillary Array Electrophoresis Genetic Analyzers for Forensic Short Tanden Repeat DNA Profiling
University of California
2004–DN–BX–K216
$821,623

mtDNA Reference Database for Domestic Dogs
George Washington University
2004–DN–BX–K004
$243,144

Nanotechnology DNA Sequencing: Improving DNA Processing Technologies
Brown University
2004–LT–BX–K001
$445,265

Palm Beach County, Florida, Continuation of DNA Program, FY 2004
Palm Beach County Sheriff's Office
2003–DN–BX–4035
$674,414

Population Genetics of Single Nucleotide Polymorphisms for Forensic Purposes
Yale University
2004–DN–BX–K025
$824,540

SpermPaint Optimization and Validation
University of Virginia
2000–IJ–CX–K013
$339,059

Validation of Y Chromosome STR Multiplexes for Operational Use
University of Central Florida
1998–IJ–CX–K003
$519,964

Forensic Casework DNA Backlog Reduction Program Formula Grants

Alabama Department of Forensic Sciences
2004–DN–BX–K149
$703,708

Alameda, County of
2004–DN–BX–K157
$147,357

Alaska Department of Public Safety
2004–DN–BX–K136
$194,620

Albuquerque, City of
2004–DN–BX–K098
$421,795

Allegheny, County of
2004–DN–BX–K085
$266,917

Anne Arundel, County of
2004–DN–BX–K156
$61,994

Arizona Criminal Justice Commission
2004–DN–BX–K040
$430,047

Arizona Department of Public Safety
2004–DN–BX–K062
$283,678

Arkansas State Crime Laboratory
2004–DN–BX–K159
$320,550

Baltimore, City of
2004–DN–BX–K059
$239,695

Bexar, County of
2004–DN–BX–K058
$146,725

Boston, City of
2004–DN–BX–K129
$33,784

Broward Sheriff's Office
2004–DN–BX–K029
$195,023

California Department of Justice
2004–DN–BX–K061
$1,065,583

Colorado Department of Public Safety
2004–DN–BX–K121
$401,291

Connecticut Department of Public Safety
2004–DN–BX–K087
$289,783

Contra Costa, County of
2004–DN–BX–K164
$165,510

Cuyahoga County Coroners Office
2004–DN–BX–K131
$52,879

Denver, City and County of
2004–DN–BX–K162
$401,873

District of Columbia Metropolitan Police
Department
2004–DN–BX–K163
$188,180

DuPage County Office of the Sheriff
2004–DN–BX–K096
$61,852

Erie, County of
2004–DN–BX–K137
$131,327

Florida Department of Law Enforcement
2004–DN–BX–K119
$1,944,178

Fresno County Sheriff's Department
2004–DN–BX–K041
$166,125

Georgia Bureau of Investigation
2004–DN–BX–K112
$970,952

Houston, City of
2004–DN–BX–K114
$509,479

Illinois State Police
2004–DN–BX–K133
$1,753,447

Indiana State Police
2004–DN–BX–K052
$788,854

Instituto De Ciencias Forenses
2004–DN–BX–K135
$363,123

Kansas Bureau of Investigation
2004–DN–BX–K139
$398,183

Kansas City Board of Police Commissioners
2004–DN–BX–K043
$216,412

Kentucky, Commonwealth of
2004–DN–BX–K130
$455,067

Kern, County of
2004–DN–BX–K044
$96,929

Las Vegas Metropolitan Police Department
2004–DN–BX–K053
$396,752

Los Angeles, City of
2004–DN–BX–K226
$669,707

Los Angeles, County of
2004–DN–BX–K084
$710,669

Louisiana State Police
2004–DN–BX–K153
$759,160

Maine Department of Public Safety
2004–DN–BX–K155
$139,883

Mansfield, City of
2004–DN–BX–K031
$130,979

Maryland State Police
2004–DN–BX–K033
$273,346

Massachusetts State Police
2004–DN–BX–K086
$663,842

Miami-Dade, County of
2004–DN–BX–K060
$410,841

Michigan, State of
2004–DN–BX–K161
$2,161,567

Minnesota, State of
2004–DN–BX–K028
$853,250

Mississippi Department of Public Safety
2004–DN–BX–K032
$497,640

Missouri State Highway Patrol
2004–DN–BX–K054
$236,981

Montana Department of Justice
2004–DN–BX–K154
$90,513

Montgomery, County of
2004–DN–BX–K046
$573,273

Montgomery, County of
2004–DN–BX–K090
$98,620

Nebraska State Patrol
2004–DN–BX–K134
$183,172

New Hampshire Department of Safety,
Division of Motor Vehicles
2004–DN–BX–K045
$163,853

New Jersey Department of Law and Public
Safety
2004–DN–BX–K092
$602,463

New York State Division of Criminal Justice
Services
2004–DN–BX–K055
$1,583,760

North Carolina Department of Crime Control
and Public Safety
2004–DN–BX–K158
$981,685

North Dakota, State of
2004–DN–BX–K217
$60,103

Northern Illinois Police Crime Laboratory
2004–DN–BX–K093
$61,852

Oakland, City of
2004–DN–BX–K051
$98,344

Ohio Office of the Attorney General
2004–DN–BX–K036
$1,151,502

Oklahoma State Bureau of Investigation
2004–DN–BX–K138
$621,066

Orange, County of
2004–DN–BX–K141
$173,440

Oregon State Police
2004–DN–BX–K049
$468,662

Palm Beach County Sheriff's Office
2004–DN–BX–K140
$191,807

Pennsylvania State Police
2004–DN–BX–K027
$223,444

Philadelphia, City of
2004–DN–BX–K088
$1,067,670

Richland County Government
2004–DN–BX–K113
$73,672

Sacramento, County of
2004–DN–BX–K035
$227,883

San Bernardino, County of
2004–DN–BX–K034
$239,504

San Diego, City of
2004–DN–BX–K118
$155,697

San Diego, County of
2004–DN–BX–K150
$180,847

San Francisco, City and County of
2004–DN–BX–K089
$143,156

San Mateo, County of
2004–DN–BX–K048
$62,326

Santa Clara, County of
2004–DN–BX–K030
$144,081

South Carolina Law Enforcement Division
2004–DN–BX–K047
$733,785

South Dakota Office of the Attorney General
2004–DN–BX–K151
$133,086

St. Louis County Police
2004–DN–BX–K057
$83,168

St. Louis Metropolitan Police Department
2004–DN–BX–K038
$105,970

Texas, State of
2004–DN–BX–K050
$1,782,700

University of North Texas Health
Science Center—Fort Worth
2004–DN–BX–K219
$371,994

Ventura, County of
2004–DN–BX–K056
$58,075

Vermont Department of Public Safety
2004–DN–BX–K039
$49,728

Virginia, Commonwealth of
2004–DN–BX–K160
$796,725

Washington State Patrol
2004–DN–BX–K095
$1,043,935

West Virginia State Police
2004–DN–BX–K026
$137,736

Wisconsin Department of Justice
2004–DN–BX–K042
$497,640

Wyoming Office of the Attorney General
2004–DN–BX–K037
$58,314

*Paul Coverdell Forensic Science
Improvement Grants*

Alabama Department of Economic and
Community Affairs
2004–DN–BX–0186
$183,075

Alaska Department of Public Safety
2004–DN–BX–0189
$57,052

Arapahoe County Sheriff's Office
2004–DN–BX–0179
$19,211

Arizona Criminal Justice Commission
2004–DN–BX–0192
$207,752

Arkansas Department of Finance and
Administration
2004–DN–BX–0185
$62,283

Baltimore, County of
2004–DN–BX–0193
$78,233

California Governor's Office of
Emergency Services
2003–DN–BX–4006
$164,668

California Governor's Office of
Emergency Services
2003–DN–BX–4077
$427,017

California Governor's Office of
Emergency Services
2004–DN–BX–0002
$89,072

California Governor's Office of
Emergency Services
2004–DN–BX–0159
$810,820

Colorado Division of Criminal Justice
2004–DN–BX–0149
$103,983

Connecticut, State of
2004–DN–BX–0148
$79,595

Dallas, County of
2004–DN–BX–0202
$80,233

Delaware Criminal Justice Council
2004–DN–BX–0180
$57,052

District of Columbia Justice
Grants Administration
2004–DN–BX–0181
$57,052

Florida Department of Law Enforcement
2004–DN–BX–0152
$388,886

Fulton, County of
2004–DN–BX–0184
$80,233

Galveston, County of, and University of
Texas Medical Branch
2004–DN–BX–0212
$80,233

Georgia Criminal Justice Coordinating Council
2004–DN–BX–0191
$276,487

Greenville County Medical Examiner
2004–DN–BX–0208
$35,233

Hamilton County Coroner
2004–DN–BX–0210
$79,175

Hawaii Department of the Attorney General
2004–DN–BX–0154
$57,052

Hernando County Sheriff's Office
2004–DN–BX–0190
$45,937

Hillsborough, County of
2004–DN–BX–0177
$72,423

Idaho State Police
2004–DN–BX–0151
$57,052

Illinois Criminal Justice Information Authority
2004–DN–BX–0194
$289,134

Indiana Criminal Justice Institute
2004–DN–BX–0153
$141,571

Iowa Governor's Office of Drug Control Policy
2004–DN–BX–0156
$67,272

Jefferson, County of
2004–DN–BX–0187
$40,234

Jefferson, County of
2004–DN–BX–0211
$78,051

Kansas, State of
2004–DN–BX–0162
$62,232

Kentucky Justice and Public Safety Cabinet
2004–DN–BX–0158
$94,092

Las Vegas Metropolitan Police Department
2004–DN–BX–0206
$80,233

Louisiana Commission on Law Enforcement
and Administration of Justice
2004–DN–BX–0195
$182,974

Maine Department of Public Safety
2004–DN–BX–0161
$57,052

Mansfield, City of
2004–DN–BX–0220
$77,233

Maryland Governor's Office of
Crime Control and Prevention
2004–DN–BX–0150
$125,879

Maryland Office of the Chief Medical Examiner
2004–DN–BX–0198
$80,083

Massachusetts State Police
2004–DN–BX–0223
$147,004

Michigan, State of
2004–DN–BX–0155
$230,328

Middlesex, County of
2004–DN–BX–0213
$80,233

Minneapolis, City of
2004–DN–BX–0199
$74,512

Minnesota Department of Public Safety
2004–DN–BX–0160
$115,607

Mississippi Department of Public Safety
2004–DN–BX–0157
$146,070

Missouri Department of Public Safety
2004–DN–BX–0163
$210,565

Montana, State of
2004–DN–BX–0168
$57,052

Montgomery, County of
2004–DN–BX–0214
$80,233

Nebraska State Patrol
2004–DN–BX–0173
$57,052

New Hampshire Department of Justice
2004–DN–BX–0209
$57,052

New Jersey Department of
Law and Public Safety
2004–DN–BX–0167
$197,387

New Mexico, State of
2004–DN–BX–0221
$57,052

New York State Division of
Criminal Justice Services
2004–DN–BX–0171
$438,494

North Carolina Governor's Crime Commission
2004–DN–BX–0170
$192,106

North Dakota, State of
2004–DN–BX–0218
$57,052

Ocean County Sheriff's Department
2004–DN–BX–0215
$70,177

Ohio Office of Criminal Justice Services
2004–DN–BX–0174
$261,308

Oklahoma District Attorneys Council
2004–DN–BX–0165
$80,239

Orange, County of
2004–DN–BX–0178
$80,233

Oregon State Police
2004–DN–BX–0205
$154,270

Pennsylvania Commission on
Crime and Delinquency
2004–DN–BX–0009
$282,550

Pinellas, County of
2004–DN–BX–0188
$52,233

Rhode Island, State of
2004–DN–BX–0222
$57,052

Savannah, City of
2004–DN–BX–0183
$76,883

South Carolina Department of Public Safety
2004–DN–BX–0166
$94,762

South Dakota Office of the Attorney General
2004–DN–BX–0203
$97,697

Spokane, County of
2004–DN–BX–0204
$73,633

St. Croix, County of
2004–DN–BX–0217
$39,750

St. Louis County Police
2004–DN–BX–0196
$80,024

Tennessee, State of
2004–DN–BX–0176
$133,484

Texas, State of
2004–DN–BX–0175
$505,408

Utah Department of Public Safety
2004–DN–BX–0216
$133,964

Ventura, County of
2004–DN–BX–0182
$80,233

Vermont Department of Public Safety
2004–DN–BX–0207
$57,052

Virgin Islands
2004–DN–BX–0201
$57,052

Virginia Department of Health
2004–DN–BX–0219
$168,778

Waco, City of
2004–DN–BX–0200
$38,733

Washington, State of
2004–DN–BX–0172
$140,104

West Virginia Division of Criminal Justice
Services
2004–DN–BX–0169
$57,052

Wisconsin Department of Justice
2004–DN–BX–0164
$125,042

Wyoming Office of the Attorney General
2004–DN–BX–0227
$57,052

LESS-LETHAL INCAPACITATION

**Collection and Dissemination of Less-Lethal
Databases to Law Enforcement**
Pennsylvania State University
2004–IJ–CX–K039
$113,481

**Compact and Rugged Pulsed Laser Technology
for Less-Lethal Weapons**
Sterling Photonics, Inc.
2004–IJ–CX–K043
$358,259

**Independent Assessment and Evaluation of
Less-Lethal Devices**
Pennsylvania State University
2004–IJ–CX–K013
$300,000

**Injuries Produced by Law Enforcement's Use
of Less-Lethal Weapons: A Multicenter Trial**
Wake Forest University Health Sciences
2004–IJ–CX–K047
$104,071

**Less-Lethal Weapon Technology Review and
Operational Needs Assessment**
Pennsylvania State University
2004–IJ–CX–K040
$202,000

**Modeling Electric Current Through
the Human Body From a Less-Lethal
Electromuscular Device**
University of Wisconsin
2004–IJ–CX–K036
$490,591

Multishot Launcher With Advanced Segmented Ring Airfoil Projectiles
Chester F. Vanek
2004–IJ–CX–K054
$350,000

Multiwave Dazzler
Scientific Applications and Research Associates, Inc.
2004–IJ–CX–K037
$419,759

Ring Airfoil Projectile System: Operational Testing Guidance
Aerospace Corporation
2004–IJ–CX–K052
$35,000

Solid-State Active Denial System Demonstration Program
Raytheon Company
2004–IJ–CX–K035
$499,995

POLICING

Blind/Sequential Police Lineup Procedures: Toward an Integrated Laboratory and Field Practice Perspective
Augsburg College
2004–IJ–CX–0044
$112,039

Conduct Needs Assessment for Personal Protective Equipment
Aspen Systems Corporation
1996–MU–MU–K011
$200,000

Enhancing Local and State Law Enforcement's Understanding and Use of Emerging Technology
International Association of Chiefs of Police
1999–LT–VX–K004
$439,820

In-Car Law Enforcement Technology
University of Houston
2003–IJ–CX–K011
$993,500

Technology Improvements for the Middle Rio Grande Region of Texas
Middle Rio Grande Development Council
2004–LT–BX–K003
$1,978,955

Testing the Effectiveness of a Comprehensive Fatigue Management Program for the Boston Police
Brigham and Women's Hospital, Inc.
2004–FS–BX–0001
$1,499,969

SCHOOLS

Evaluation of the "Bully-Proofing Your School" Program
University of Colorado
2004–IJ–CX–0082
$406,361

Safe Schools, Law Enforcement, and Corrections Research Support
George Mason University
2000–RD–CX–K003
$49,815

Teacher-Parent Authentication Security System II: The Next Generation of Iris Recognition Technology in Schools
Freehold Borough Board of Education
2004–RD–CX–K003
$369,998

TECHNOLOGY

Design and Development of the Predator and Prey Alert System
Florida State University
2004–RD–CX–K154
$280,998

Effects of Radio Frequency (RF) Radiation on Motor Vehicles Due to Variations in the Polarization and Frequency of RF Waveforms
Eureka Aerospace
2004–IJ–CX–K044
$188,444

Kentucky Community Critical Infrastructure Protection Laboratory
Eastern Kentucky University
2004–IJ–CX–K055
$5,000,000

Northeast Technology and Product Assessment Committee
Massachusetts Department of Correction
2004–LT–BX–K086
$50,000

Project SeaHawk, Phase II
South Carolina Research Authority
2002–MU–MU–K011
$7,421,081

**Wireless and Rapid Deployment
Upgrades to ShotSpotter System**
South Carolina Research Authority
2002–MU–MU–K011
$890,530

*Technology, National Law Enforcement
and Corrections Technology Centers*

**Development of the National
Corrections and Law Enforcement
Training and Technology Center**
National Corrections and Law Enforcement
Training and Technology Center
2001–LT–BX–K007
$989,477

**Law Enforcement and Corrections
Technology Commercialization**
Office of Law Enforcement Technology
Commercialization, Inc.
2003–IJ–CX–K001
$3,148,280

**National Law Enforcement and Corrections
Technology Center—Rocky Mountain Region**
University of Denver—Colorado Seminary
1996–MU–MU–K012
$2,971,432

**National Law Enforcement and Corrections
Technology Center—Southeast Crime Series
Analysis Project**
South Carolina Research Authority
2002–MU–MU–K011
$250,000

**Operations of the National Law Enforcement
and Corrections Technology Center**
Aspen Systems Corporation
1996–MU–MU–K011
$2,896,432

**Operations of the National Law Enforcement
and Corrections Technology Center—
Southeast Region**
South Carolina Research Authority
2002–MU–MU–K011
$2,846,432

**Operations of the National Law Enforcement
and Corrections Technology Center—
Western Region**
Aerospace Corporation
2000–MU–MU–K004
$2,875,040

Rural Law Enforcement Technology Center
Eastern Kentucky University
2001–MU–MU–K009
$2,643,449

TERRORISM AND CRITICAL
INCIDENTS

**Counterterrorism Preparedness for
International and Domestic Police
Forces and Research at the Center on
Terrorism at John Jay College**
City University of New York
2004–DB–BX–1010
$247,369

**16x20 Inch Instant Film X-Ray
System for Bomb Technicians**
Wisner Classic Manufacturing Company, Inc.
2003–RD–CX–K012
$20,000

**Technical Considerations for Effective Policy to
Implement Chemical and Biological Detectors
for First Responders and Law Enforcement**
Monterey Institute of International Studies
2004–IJ–CX–0050
$283,589

VICTIMIZATION AND VICTIM
SERVICES

**Court Responses to Batterer Program
Noncompliance: A National Perspective**
Fund for the City of New York
2004–WG–BX–0005
$142,631

**Evaluation of Services for Trafficking
Victims Discretionary Grant Program:
Comprehensive Service Site**
Caliber Associates, Inc.
2002–MU–MU–K004
$162,641

**Impact of Proactive Enforcement of
No-Contact Orders on Victim Safety**
University of South Carolina
Research Foundation
2004–WG–BX–0007
$446,542

**Law Enforcement Response to Human
Trafficking and the Implications for Victims**
Caliber Associates, Inc.
2004–WG–BX–0088
$199,661

**Mandatory Reporting of Nursing Home
Deaths: Markers for Mistreatment, Effect on
Care Quality, and Generalizability**
University of Missouri
2004–IJ–CX–1012
$432,061

**Preventing Repeat Incidents of Family
Violence: A Randomized Multi-Site Field Test**
Police Foundation
2004–WG–BX–0002
$411,961

Stages of Change and the Group Treatment of Batterers
BOTEC Analysis Corporation
2004–WG–BX–0011
$78,391

VIOLENCE

Firearms

Child-Safe Personalized Weapons: Smart Gun Project
New Jersey, State of
2004–IJ–CX–0096
$1,133,941

Crime Gun Risk Factors: Impact of Dealer, Firearm, Transaction, and Buyer Characteristics on the Likelihood of Gun Use in Crime
University of Pennsylvania
2004–IJ–CX–0030
$103,514

Strategic Disruption of Firearms Markets: Evaluation of the Utility of the Bureau of Alcohol, Tobacco, Firearms, and Explosives' Youth Crime Gun Interdiction Initiative
Rand Corporation
2001–IJ–CX–0028
$249,877

Sexual Assault

Characteristics, Processes, and Outcomes of Sexual Assaults in Alaska
University of Alaska
2004–WG–BX–0003
$152,087

Development of an Online Domestic Violence and Sexual Assault Data Resource Center
Justice Research and Statistics Association, Inc.
2004–WG–BX–0012
$224,131

Impact of Self-Protection on Rape and Injury
Florida State University
2004–IJ–CX–0046
$33,825

Prevalence, Context, and Reporting of Drug-Facilitated Sexual Assault on University Campuses
Research Triangle Institute
2004–WG–BX–0010
$419,339

Visiting Fellowship Program: Police Investigations of Rape— Roadblocks and Solutions
Ohio University
2003–IJ–CX–1027
$166,089

Violence Against Women and Family Violence

Center on Domestic Violence, University of Colorado—Denver Graduate School of Public Affairs
University of Colorado—Denver
2004–DD–BX–1005
$742,108

Domestic Violence Digital Evidence
New York, City of
2004–RG–CX–K005
$397,400

Effects of Different Case Screening Practices on Domestic Violence Recidivism
Safe Horizon
2004–WG–BX–0009
$433,942

Effects of Intimate Partner Violence on the Workplace
University of Arkansas
2003–RD–CX–0021
$247,369

Impact of a Specialized Domestic Violence Police Unit
University of North Carolina—Charlotte
2004–WG–BX–0004
$93,878

Offender Characteristics, Offense Mix, and Escalation in Domestic Violence
University of Florida
2004–IJ–CX–0013
$24,856

Preventing Firearm Violence Among Victims of Intimate Partner Violence: Evaluation of a New North Carolina Law
Pacific Institute for Research and Evaluation
2004–IJ–CX–0025
$114,784

Stages of Change and the Group Treatment of Batterers
University of Pennsylvania
2004–WG–BX–0001
$236,176

Year Five Evaluation of a Multisite Demonstration of Collaborations to Address Domestic Violence and Child Maltreatment
Caliber Associates, Inc.
2000–MU–MU–0014
$549,967

WEAPONS TECHNOLOGY

Multifunctional Grenade Modeling and Simulation
Scientific Applications and Research Associates, Inc.
2004–IJ–CX–K051
$149,917

SECURES® Demonstration in Hampton/ Newport News, Virginia
Planning Systems, Inc.
2003–IJ–CX–K029
$248,989

YOUTH

AMBERVIEW: Digitally Recording and Storing 3-D Facial Images and Fingerprints of School-Age Children
West Virginia High Technology Consortium Foundation
2004–LT–BX–K002
$494,739

Childhood Maltreatment and Pathways to Delinquency
National Institute for Law and Equity
2004–JL–FX–1064
$98,948

Long-Term Effects of After-School Programming on Educational Adjustment and Juvenile Crime: A Study of Los Angeles' BEST After-School Program
University of California
2004–SI–FX–0032
$522,576

Trajectories of Violent Offending and Risk Status Across Adolescence and Early Adulthood
Portland State University
2004–IJ–CX–0017
$35,000

Volunteer Child Mentoring: Effects of Same-Race Compared to Cross-Race Matching
New York University
2004–JG–FX–1007
$130,000

Appendix C
NIJ Publications and Products in FY 2004

Most NIJ materials are free and can be obtained from these three sources:

1. NIJ Web page: http://www.ojp.usdoj.gov/nij.

2. National Criminal Justice Reference Service (NCJRS): http://www.ncjrs.org, 800–851–3420, P.O. Box 6000, Rockville, MD 20849–6000.

3. National Law Enforcement and Corrections Technology Center (NLECTC) (for science and technology materials): http://www.justnet.org, 800–248–2742.

CHILD ABUSE AND NEGLECT

A Resource for Evaluating Child Advocacy Centers, Jackson, Shelly L., Special Report, July 2004, 414 pages, NCJ 192825.

CORRECTIONS

Duress Systems in Corrections Facilities, National Institute of Justice, In Short—Toward Criminal Justice Solutions, September 2004, 3 pages, NCJ 205836.

COURTS, PROSECUTION, AND DEFENSE

Fighting Urban Crime: The Evolution of Federal-Local Collaboration, Russell-Einhorn, Malcolm L., Research in Brief, December 2003, 19 pages, NCJ 197040.

Science and the Law: 2001 and 2002 National Conferences, National Institute of Justice, Special Report, May 2004, 86 pages, NCJ 202955.

CRIME CONTROL

Characteristics of Chinese Human Smugglers, Zhang, Sheldon, and Ko-lin Chin, Research in Brief, August 2004, 19 pages, NCJ 204989.

Evaluating G.R.E.A.T.: A School-Based Gang Prevention Program, Esbensen, Finn-Aage, Research for Policy, June 2004, 7 pages, NCJ 198604.

Fighting Urban Crime: The Evolution of Federal-Local Collaboration, Russell-Einhorn, Malcolm L., Research in Brief, December 2003, 19 pages, NCJ 197040.

Gambling and Crime Among Arrestees: Exploring the Link, McCorkle, Richard C., Research for Practice, July 2004, 13 pages, NCJ 203197.

NIJ Journal, No. 250, National Institute of Justice, November 2003, 53 pages, JR 000250.

NIJ Journal, No. 251, National Institute of Justice, July 2004, 35 pages, JR 000251.

CYBER/ELECTRONIC CRIME

Forensic Examination of Digital Evidence: A Guide for Law Enforcement, National Institute of Standards and Technology, Special Report, April 2004, 101 pages, NCJ 199408.

Test Results for Software Write Block Tools: RCMP HDL VO.4, National Institute of Justice, Special Report, August 2004, 83 pages, NCJ 206231.

Test Results for Software Write Block Tools: RCMP HDL VO.5, National Institute of Justice, Special Report, August 2004, 82 pages, NCJ 206232.

Test Results for Software Write Block Tools: RCMP HDL VO.7, National Institute of Justice, Special Report, August 2004, 85 pages, NCJ 206233.

Test Results for Software Write Block Tools: RCMP HDL VO.8, National Institute of Justice, Special Report, February 2004, 86 pages, NCJ 203196.

DRUGS, ALCOHOL, AND CRIME

Fighting Urban Crime: The Evolution of Federal-Local Collaboration, Russell-Einhorn, Malcolm L., Research in Brief, December 2003, 19 pages, NCJ 197040.

Gambling and Crime Among Arrestees: Exploring the Link, McCorkle, Richard C., Research for Practice, July 2004, 13 pages, NCJ 203197.

NIJ Journal, No. 250, National Institute of Justice, November 2003, 53 pages, JR 000250.

EXPLOSIVE DETECTION/REMEDIATION

Vanguard Robot Assessment, National Institute of Justice, In Short—Toward Criminal Justice Solutions, July 2004, 5 pages, NCJ 204637.

INVESTIGATIVE AND FORENSIC SCIENCES

Crime Scene Investigation: A Reference for Law Enforcement Training, Technical Working Group on Crime Scene Investigation, Special Report, June 2004, 69 pages, NCJ 200160.

Education and Training in Forensic Science: A Guide for Forensic Science Laboratories, Educational Institutions, and Students, Technical Working Group for Education and Training in Forensic Science, Special Report, June 2004, 64 pages, NCJ 203099.

Science and the Law: 2001 and 2002 National Conferences, National Institute of Justice, Special Report, May 2004, 86 pages, NCJ 202955.

POLICING

Español for Law Enforcement: An Interactive Training Tool, National Institute of Justice, February 2004, CD–ROM, NCJ 201801.

Hiring and Keeping Police Officers, National Institute of Justice and Office of Community Oriented Policing Services, Research for Practice, July 2004, 14 pages, NCJ 202289.

Law Enforcement Technology: Are Small and Rural Agencies Equipped and Trained? National Institute of Justice, Research for Practice, June 2004, 14 pages, NCJ 204609.

Voice Translators for Law Enforcement, National Institute of Justice, In Short—Toward Criminal Justice Solutions, September 2004, 4 pages, NCJ 205837.

SURVEILLANCE AND DETECTION

Hand-Held Metal Detectors for Use in Concealed Weapon and Contraband Detection (NIJ Standard-0602.02), Paulter, Jr., Nicholas G., NIJ Standard, November 2003, 55 pages, NCJ 200330.

VICTIMIZATION

NIJ Journal, No. 250, National Institute of Justice, November 2003, 53 pages, JR 000250.

A Resource for Evaluating Child Advocacy Centers, Jackson, Shelly L., Special Report, July 2004, 414 pages, NCJ 192825.

VIOLENCE AND VIOLENT CRIME

NIJ Journal, No. 250, National Institute of Justice, November 2003, 53 pages, JR 000250.

When Violence Hits Home: How Economics and Neighborhood Play a Role, Benson, Michael L., and Greer Litton Fox, Research in Brief, September 2004, 12 pages, NCJ 205004.

NIJ JOURNAL

NIJ Journal, No. 250, National Institute of Justice, November 2003, 53 pages, JR 000250.

NIJ Journal, No. 251, National Institute of Justice, July 2004, 35 pages, JR 000251.

ANNUAL REPORTS

NIJ 2002 Annual Report, National Institute of Justice, Annual Report to Congress, January 2004, 43 pages, NCJ 200338.

Top Publications by Number of Electronic Copies Accessed from the Web, FY 2004

Title and Author	Accessed	Accessed	NCJ Number	Year Published
Electronic Crime Scene Investigation: A Guide for First Responders (Guide), NIJ	103,240	http://www.ncjrs.org/pdffiles1/nij/187736.pdf	NCJ 187736	2001
Crime Scene Investigation:				
• *A Guide for Law Enforcement* (Research Report), NIJ	98,658	http://www.ncjrs.org/pdffiles1/nij/178280.pdf	NCJ 178280	2000
• *A Reference for Law Enforcement Training* (Special Report), NIJ	73,631	http://www.ncjrs.org/pdffiles1/nij/200160.pdf	NCJ 200160	2004
Eyewitness Evidence:				
• *A Trainer's Manual for Law Enforcement* (Special Report), NIJ	74,392	http://www.ncjrs.org/nij/eyewitness/188678.pdf	NCJ 188678	2003
• *A Guide for Law Enforcement* (Research Report), NIJ	50,579	http://www.ncjrs.org/pdffiles1/nij/178240.pdf	NCJ 178240	1999
Forensic Examination of Digital Evidence: A Guide for Law Enforcement (Special Report), NIJ	72,464	http://www.ncjrs.org/pdffiles1/nij/199408.pdf	NCJ 199408	2004
Death Investigation: A Guide for the Scene Investigator (Research Report),NIJ, Bureau of Justice Assistance, and Centers for Disease Control and Prevention	65,709	http://www.ncjrs.org/pdffiles/167568.pdf	NCJ 167568	1999
The Sexual Victimization of College Women (Research Report), Bonnie S. Fischer, Francis T. Cullen, and Michael G. Turner	63,739	http://www.ncjrs.org/pdffiles1/nij/182369.pdf	NCJ 182369	2000
Using DNA to Solve Cold Cases (Special Report), NIJ	60,301	http://www.ncjrs.org/pdffiles1/nij/194197.pdf	NCJ 194197	2002
Guide for the Selection of Personal Protective Equipment for Emergency First Responders, NIJ Guide 102-00, Volume I (Guide), Alim A. Fatah, John A. Barrett, Richard D. Arcilesi, Jr., Charlotte H. Lattin, Charles G. Janney, and Edward A. Blackman	60,164	http://www.ncjrs.org/pdffiles1/nij/191518.pdf	NCJ 191518	2002
Education and Training in Forensic Science: A Guide for Forensic Science Laboratories, Educational Institutions, and Students (Special Report), NIJ	59,472	http://www.ncjrs.org/pdffiles1/nij/203099.pdf	NCJ 203099	2004
Arrestee Drug Abuse Monitoring: 2000 Annual Report (Research Report), NIJ	58,844	http://www.ncjrs.org/pdffiles1/nij/193013.pdf	NCJ 193013	2003
Responding to Gangs: Evaluation and Research (Research Report), Winifred L. Reed and Scott H. Decker, eds.	54,844	http://www.ncjrs.org/pdffiles1/nij/190351.pdf	NCJ 190351	2002
Extent, Nature, and Consequences of Intimate Partner Violence: Findings From the National Violence Against Women Survey (Research Report), Patricia Tjaden and Nancy Thoennes	53,897	http://www.ncjrs.org/pdffiles1/nij/181867.pdf	NCJ 181867	2000
Guide for the Selection of Chemical Agent and Toxic Industrial Material Detection Equipment for Emergency First Responders, NIJ Guide 100-00, Volume 1 (Guide), Alim A. Fatah, Richard D. Arcilesi, Jr., Kenneth J. Ewing, Charlotte H. Lattin, and Michael S. Helinski	51,366	http://www.ncjrs.org/pdffiles1/nij/184449.pdf	NCJ 184449	2000
Full Report of the Prevalence, Incidence, and Consequences of Violence Against Women: Findings From the National Violence Against Women Survey (Research Report), Patricia Tjaden and Nancy Thoennes	41,038	http://www.ncjrs.org/pdffiles1/nij/183781.pdf	NCJ 183781	2000
Batterer Intervention Programs: Where Do We Go From Here? (Special Report), Shelly Jackson, Lynette Feder, David R. Forde, Robert C. Davis, Christopher D. Maxwell, and Bruce G. Taylor	37,510	http://www.ncjrs.org/pdffiles1/nij/195079.pdf	NCJ 195079	2003
Use of Force by Police: Overview of National and Local Data (Research Report), Kenneth Adams, Geoffrey P. Alpert, Roger G. Dunham, Joel H. Garner, Lawrence A. Greenfeld, Mark A. Henriquez, Patrick A. Langan, Christopher D. Maxwell, and Steven K. Smith	37,345	http://www.ncjrs.org/pdffiles1/nij/176330-1.pdf	NCJ 176330	1999
An Introduction to Biological Agent Detection Equipment for Emergency First Responders, NIJ Guide 101-00 (Guide), Alim A. Fatah, John A. Barrett, Richard D. Arcilesi, Jr., Kenneth J. Ewing, Charlotte H. Lattin, and Timothy F. Moshier	34,785	http://www.ncjrs.org/pdffiles1/nij/190747.pdf	NCJ 190747	2001
Addressing Correctional Officer Stress: Programs and Strategies (Issues and Practices), Peter Finn	34,610	http://www.ncjrs.org/pdffiles1/nij/183474.pdf	NCJ 183474	2000

Top Publications by Number of Paper Copies Requested, FY 2004

Title and Author	Quantity	NCJ Number	Year Published
Español for Law Enforcement: An Interactive Tool (CD–ROM), NIJ	7,117	NCJ 201801	2004
What Every Law Enforcement Officer Should Know About DNA Evidence, NIJ			
• Brochure	6,662	NCJ 204892	1999
• Beginning module #1 (CD–ROM)	4,396	NCJ 182992	2000
• Advanced module #2 (CD–ROM)	5,431	NCJ 184479	2000
Crime Scene Investigation: A Guide for Law Enforcement (Research Report), NIJ	4,772	NCJ 178280	2000
Conflict Resolution for School Personnel: An Interactive School Safety Training Tool (CD–ROM), NIJ	4,629	NCJ 194198	2002
Death Investigation: A Guide for the Scene Investigator (Research Report), NIJ, Bureau of Justice Assistance, and Centers for Disease Control and Prevention	4,574	NCJ 167568	1999
Crime in the Schools: Reducing Conflict with Student Problem Solving (Research in Brief), Dennis J. Kenney and Steuart Watson	4,375	NCJ 177618	1999
Eyewitness Evidence:			
• *A Guide for Law Enforcement* (Research Report), NIJ	3,319	NCJ 178240	1999
• *A Trainer's Manual for Law Enforcement* (Special Report), NIJ	3,280	NCJ 188678	2003
Using DNA to Solve Cold Cases (Special Report), NIJ	3,258	NCJ 194197	2002
Emergency Responder Chemical and Biological Equipment Guides and Database (CD–ROM), NIJ	3,011	NCJ 197978	2003
Understanding DNA Evidence: A Guide for Victim Service Providers (Brochure), NIJ and Office for Victims of Crime	2,931	NCJ 185690	2001
Guide for Explosion and Bombing Scene Investigation (Research Report), NIJ	2,772	NCJ 181869	2000
Advancing Justice Through DNA Technology (Online Document), White House	2,312	NCJ 200005	2003
Forensic Examination of Digital Evidence: A Guide for Law Enforcement (Special Report), NIJ	2,300	NCJ 199408	2004
Fire and Arson Scene Evidence: A Guide for Public Safety Personnel (Research Report), Brian M. Dixon and Ronald L. Kelly, eds.	2,260	NCJ 181584	2000
NIJ Journal, No. 250 (Cover story on Intimate Partner Violence), NIJ	2,034	NCJ 196543	2003
Do Batterer Intervention Programs Work? Two Studies (Research for Practice), NIJ	1,914	NCJ 200331	2003
Responding to Gangs: Evaluation and Research (Research Report), Winifred L. Reed and Scott H. Decker, eds.	1,618	NCJ 190351	2002
Report to the Attorney General on Delays in Forensic DNA Analysis (Special Report), NIJ	1,579	NCJ 199425	2003
Factors That Influence Public Opinion of the Police (Research for Practice), Cheryl Maxson, Karen Hennigan, and David C. Sloane	1,491	NCJ 197925	2003